an elf's journey

HEALING CHILDHOOD SEXUAL ABUSE

an elf's journey

HEALING CHILDHOOD SEXUAL ABUSE

FOR TEENS AND BEYOND, AND SUPPORTERS OF SURVIVORS

Katia Cooper

Praise for *An Elf's Journey*...

An Elf's Journey is a story that I would recommend to my clients healing from childhood sexual abuse. Katia's constructive imagination is a wonderful and needed resource to traditional therapy. This book will give me a gentle place to start and also, guide the process for the progress of my client. The thoroughness of the emotions covered comprises all the feelings survivors experience from the many aspects of abuse. There is not another guide for trauma survivors to engage with in such a creative way that is required to recover wholeness. I really like the tools provided along the way. Although all people might not be willing to try certain things, I love the progression of important and necessary tools like grounding, breathing, meditation, journaling, parts work, and so forth. I also love how the suggested healing emphasizes the importance of creating and having a safe space. I envision how helpful this book will be in group therapy, too. **An Elf's Journey** *is wonderful.*

~ JODIE ELLIS-HART, LCSW
Milwaukee, WI

Kudos to you for this — and I love the spirit with which you approach healing through imagination, play, creativity, etc.

~ RACHEL GRANT, M.A. Counseling Psychology,
Sexual Abuse Recovery Coach
San Francisco, CA

As I was falling asleep one night, thinking about the characters in **An Elf's Journey**, *I realized I had fallen in love with them. I had felt their shame when they spoke the truth and weren't believed. My heart sang when they courageously stepped into their healing journey. Anyone who has experienced inappropriate touching will identify with the characters'* *ongoing struggles with fear and trust issues, experience aha moments in their own healing journey, and begin to understand their family's reactions to disclosure.*

~ Marilyn M. Hein, MA, LPC,
Hearts Unfolding Counseling, Oshkosh WI

This book sets the stage for real healing and magic to happen. I can't wait to read the rest!

~ Sybil Kleinmichel, Executive Coach and Author
Frankfurt, Germany

I love this story! It made me feel so much less alone and so much more alert to what childhood should have felt like and how mine went astray. I appreciate how it is real enough for a child or adult to touch the truth of those painful moments and memories without being too physical in the descriptions. It told what happened without being overly jarring... it brought in the light and that was precious to me. I have been losing my way, but **An Elf's Journey** *reminded me that it is ok to take time when I am feeling unsure. It was a reminder to just breathe and be. The story provided an example to talk with my neglected and hurting parts, and to let them have a voice. I truly found this a precious thing.*

~From a Survivor and Art Therapist

This is one of the best explorations of childhood trauma and its effect on a person's psyche that I have ever seen. The author has done a wonderful job shedding light on this complex and difficult subject. I am really inspired and impressed. Using metaphorical characters, including faeries and woodland creatures, Cooper tells a story of abuse, personal healing, and then healing of an entire community from the trauma of sexual abuse, through open dialogue, creating safe spaces, creativity, connection with the earth, and many other real-life therapeutic techniques. This book is a must read for survivors and practitioners alike, as well as anyone who is interested in helping others move forward from trauma.

~ Sarah Symons, Founder and Executive Director
of MadeBySurvivors and Relevee

You showed that there was life before the harm, and that we can rekindle that joyful elf spirit within to be one with nature and soft gentle things that life holds—waiting for us when we are ready. My spirit had ached for wilderness and green connection that I re-kindled in experiencing this story! Thank you so much Katia for this gift you are sharing with me and others. Sincerely... it has meant so much to me.

~ Survivor/Thriver

An inspiring journey that gives the reader the space to look at their past from a different perspective, change energies and transform trauma.

- Bettina Madini, Artist, Singer, Writer, Change Agent

With playful power, An Elf's Journey provides a place for a broad range of ages to explore processing the trauma of a child's broken trust. Katia Cooper uses an authentic rhythm within her words to gently unfold room to be curious, when healing a body violation can feel difficult to imagine. She encourages us to believe that while trauma processing can be eccentric and dense, we can breathe into the mystery by befriending intelligent and dedicated fairies. Fairies that can support us to discover light in our bodies, and weave light around us so a new culture of care can emerge.

~ Sara Daleiden, Artist and Director, MKE<->LAX

AN ELF'S JOURNEY

Copyright 2017©Katia Cooper

ISBN 978-0-9983708-8-0

Cover & Interior Design by Roseanna White

Original cover background and the digital magic of interior drawings by Katia Cooper.

Additionally, Bettina Madini is the artist who digitally painted the tree, the fairy, and the tiny elf in the pod to Katia's Process Art project.

First Edition

No part of this publication may be translated, reproduced, or transmitted in any form without prior permission in writing from the author, except in the case of brief quotations, with credit to the author.

Product names or trademarks mentioned in this publication remain property of their respective owners.

This book is not intended as a substitute for the advice of health practitioners. If you have concerns about any suggestions or exercises, please consult your inner wisdom and/or a health professional for choosing what is right for you.

Published by Happy Publishing, www.HappyPublishing.net

Dedication

*To the Inner Child of those who have endured
childhood trauma that was left unresolved.
I dedicate this book to your process
of discovering your unique gifts
and the magic of your authentic Self.*

Table of Contents

NOTE TO THE READER..15

CHAPTER ~ 1 ~ Mmm Mmm Mmmmm~Magical Story!......................17

CHAPTER ~ 2 ~ Haunting Events..21

CHAPTER ~ 3 ~ Inside a Shell...29

    Shifting Feelings...33

CHAPTER ~ 4 ~ Transparent Wings..34

CHAPTER ~ 5 ~ Guardian of Undercover Treasures......................37

CHAPTER ~ 6~ Treasured Friendship...45

CHAPTER ~ 7 ~ Meeting the Fairapist..49

    Self-Care for Trauma or Overwhelming Fear........................50

CHAPTER ~ 8 ~ Melting the Trauma...56

    Exercise to Calm the Panic..57

CHAPTER ~9~ Inner Repairs..61

CHAPTER ~ 10 ~ Accessing Creativity and Logic..........................65
    Using Your Left Brain and Right Brain for Trauma Relief..67
    Accessing Left Brain Traits...67
    Using Your Right Brain for Relief...68
    Using Creativity and Logic..70
    Using Your Left and Right Brain—Summary......................71

CHAPTER ~ 11 ~ Transformation: The Art of Meditation............73
    A Protective Practice..76

CHAPTER ~ 12 ~ Elf's Self Aligned with Source............................80

CHAPTER ~ 13 ~ Detachment to Resolve the Pain........................84

CHAPTER ~ 14 ~ Gifts of Self...88
    Unwrapping More..91

CHAPTER ~ 15 ~ Shell's Pain Needs an Outlet..............................95
    Unlimited Heart..99
    Replacing Judgment with Curiosity.....................................100
    Wanting to Die..101

CHAPTER ~ 16 ~ Emerging Butterfly!...104

CHAPTER ~ 17 ~ New Beginning...110

CHAPTER ~ 18 ~ Elf's Plight and Purpose..................................115

CHAPTER ~ 19 ~ Centering—Calm Focusing..............................121
    Centering...123

CHAPTER ~ 20 ~ SELF-ASSURANCE, SIMPLIFYING, and CLARITY.........126

    SELF-ASSURANCE...127

    ASSISTANCE TO SUPPORT YOUR INNER ELF OR FAIRY....................129

    SIMPLIFY..130

    CLARITY..131

CHAPTER ~ 21 ~ HANDS-ON-HEALING..133

    COURAGE..135

    JULIO'S POWER ANIMAL PLAY...138

CHAPTER ~ 22 ~ WATER SPIRITS..140

    ELF FEELS TORN...142

CHAPTER ~ 23 ~ COMFORT AND BELONGING.....................................148

    BELONGING...149

    SOURCE, RADIATING TO SELF AND ELF......................................150

    COMFORT..151

    LETTER TO MY YOUNGER elfie..152

CHAPTER ~ 24 ~ LIGHTEN UP...153

    LOVING LAUGHTER..153

    APPROPRIATE TIME FOR LAUGHTER..154

CHAPTER ~ 25 ~ THE WELCOMED END..158

    ABOUT EMPOWERMENT..161

REFERENCES...163

RESOURCES..163

ABOUT THE COVER ARTIST..164

ACKNOWLEDGEMENTS..165

Note to the Reader...

MMMmmmmmmmmm! Stories can bring warm fuzzies to the eyes and ears of your heart. They can create smiles and pictures for your mind. Tales may show a problem and spark your imagination to find a resolve or create a dream. Even cartoons can display dilemmas to stimulate creative thinking. When you see a story or a play, *soulutions* and brilliant ideas can become apparent for your own life. Your creativity dreams up new ways to become free of burdens. As you step into life with a new view, your soles take you on a journey to integrate a new story for your soul. There is truly a soul purpose for the places your soles take you. Maybe that is what makes a story magical and believable at the same time!

Chapter ~ 1 ~

MmmMmmMmmmm~Magical Story!

Once upon a time, there was a very bright spirited elf. She had a glow that was noticed by those who really observed. The glow came from more than the smile on the little elf's face. The young elf was really good at having fun, as songs of delight often accompanied her fluent bouncy steps!

There were some odd habits, unfortunately, that the elf's mother handed down to her. One of them was the way she spelled elf's name, without capitalizing the first letter. Her name was elf, with a small "e". elf's mother thought poorly of herself and without realizing it, she did not want to give attention to the importance of elf. It did not appear to affect elf when she was little. In fact, elf's glimmering spirit brightened her mother's day to day life.

elf played as if joy was the main design or purpose for her. She played carefree without worries. And life was pretty good. The youthful sprout had lots of friends and they played all kinds of games. elf frolicked with fairies, frogs, toads, birds, and even bugs. When she played with animals in the woods, the squirrels and bunnies gave rides to her and her friends. They had to hold on tight so they wouldn't fall off. The little critters knew just how fast to go to keep their tiny passengers on board. They were able to put the needs of the young ones first, like considerate babysitters, and they respected the fairy realm.

The graceful trees in the forest were also friends of the elf and fairy folk. They stood strong for the wee ones. The fairy realm built forts and homes in the trunks and the exposed roots. Lush greens became streamers and garlands, and the moss made a plush carpet. Sticks were constructed into simple furniture and ladders. The fluffy white floss attached to milkweed and dandelion seeds were stuffed into leaves, which were sewn together for cushions. All needs were provided for. The charmed elves, fairies, and creatures lived in harmony with nature.

elf also made games out of her chores. She delighted in gathering nuts and berries with her friends. They would often trade what they collected so they could get their favorites. elf's favorites were hazelnuts and mulberries. She would give the fairies the blueberries and raspberries that grew low to the ground in exchange for the mulberries that were easy for the fairies to pluck high in the trees.

At home, elf would pretend to be a cleaning fairy when she swept the ground or tidied up. She knew that a clean environment pleased the fairies, so she pulled in that energy of delight to create an orderly space.

Much of nature joined forces to help one another. The leaves provided sun-dappled designs as the fairy realm added color to the flowers. Life was comfortable and elf felt safe. Delightful music by crickets, frogs, and birds filled the air. Everything around her and inside her danced with enchantment.

In the land of fairies, elves can be charming characters. They have a physical body similar to humans though they tend to be very small in comparison. Usually their features are dainty and adorable. Pointy ears, full cheeks, button noses, and big eyes are common.

Elves love to help others. Some elves wish to become heroes or sheroes—female heroes—to make the world a better place. Elves have large hearts and tremendous, TREMENDOUS spirits! They do not want to give up. Elves have an inner strength and belief that makes them determined to do just what is needed to make a contribution to enhance the world. A spirited elf is a wonderful and admirable creature.

The heart center of an elf carries the design for the fullest potential in his or her life. This heart design is made up of beautiful layers. In traveling through the layers, elves remember the key to loving their elf Self. The journey can become complicated when the natural order is disrupted by traumatic situations which require elves to dig deeper into their heart and spirit to know the value they have in this world. The spirit is what makes each Being unique and different from anyone else.

Elves and fairies are also known as "nature spirits" or the "fairy realm." Many youngins tend to be cared for by nature, including community more than their birth families. As nature spirits grow emotionally, mentally, and spiritually, they assist humans as they grow. If people understand this, they can open themselves to the hope that these nature spirits offer.

Fairies are different than elves because they have wings. Some fairies have transparent wings like dragonflies and others have butterfly-like extensions; their wings are not like the feather wings of birds and angels. A trickle of them have multihued, translucent wings that glitter with moonlight. Fairies can fly and are sometimes called "earth angels". Their egos can make them opinionated, unlike "heavenly angels" who provide unconditional love.

These nature spirits can be visible to sensitive humans as small glowing lights that float as orbs. They can take on different forms, orbs being their clearest state.

Fairies tend to be caring beings with the mission to protect the environment and animals. They reward people for their kindness and care toward others, animals, nature, and surroundings. Fairies will respond to requests for help from humans and elves. A fairy may test them to ensure they are reliable guardians of the earth. Fairies are light, fun, airy beings. They remind us to lighten up and not take life too seriously. They help awaken creativity, space, joy, and a sense of accomplishment.

Fairies are connected to the elements in nature such as air, water, fire, and earth. They blend with nature and influence the elements and wildlife more than elves. Fairies can also be wilder. Their essence and feelings are expressed through nature. Joy could be reflected in a flower, sadness through a rainstorm, or hope through a rainbow.

Elves tend to only commune with nature. They have taken on more of a solid physical body, somewhat similar to humans.

Long ago, the fairy realm essentially made themselves invisible to survive the threats of the human race. Make no mistake though, they are more potent than ever after veiling their presence. Potency multiplies in strength when it is forced into secrecy by exclusion from those who take advantage of misusing power. It takes a high vibration and curious nature to sense the nature spirits. Children and nature lovers are frequently in touch with them.

Let's return to the life of the sweet, happy elf. She enjoyed a stress-free existence until haunting events stole her security before she was even old enough to go to school.

Chapter ~ 2 ~

Haunting Events

At home, elf had parents who cared well for her and her little brother, Bevin, until a sad incident halted the family connection they enjoyed. Her mother lost a baby before it was born. elf did not understand her own feelings, because her parents did not want to talk about their feelings or acknowledge their loss.

Sorely, Mother Elf would nitpick nonstop. She would often holler, "You can't do anything right!" As much as Father Elf tried to please Mother Elf, she snapped at him, and he retreated into a helpless place. It was as if the safe, emotionally calm waters that elf joyfully thrived in had turned to jagged ice in the little elf shack. She had no way to know the past secrets that both parents kept hidden, or that they secretly blamed themselves when they had strong emotions, which added to their shame. The shame kept the ice solid so no one could help.

It felt lonely in her home, like important elements were missing. Her mother often slept much of the day and seemed angry when she was awake. The loving elvish ways of elf's mother had vanished. Both of elf's parents stopped paying attention to her like they used to. They always seemed too busy and troubled within themselves to tend to elf. Her parents' adorable elf-like characteristics faded.

Adding to elf's sadness, Grandmother Elf was critical of her grown daughter—elf's mother. She believed everyone should act happy and not show sorrow. So, Mother Elf ignored her hurt feelings; she tried to act the way her mother expected her to act because she wanted her mother to accept her. However, she seemed depressed and got overly mad with her children about small things.

Grandma Elf nagged her daughter about her body, "If you wouldn't eat so much, you wouldn't be so heavy and lazy. That's what makes you so unhappy!" elf would pull her shoulders up to her ears, not wanting to hear more of what offended her mother's feelings. She felt sorry for her mother when her grandma was so unkind. She was baffled that her mother would not speak up for herself.

elf and Bevin would visit their grandma and grandpa, who were often painfully preoccupied with arguing when they were together. It wasn't this way when they were apart from each other. When together, they lost the magic of life and appeared more human than the darling elves she knew them to be. When Grandma Elf was alone with elf, she would teach elf how to garden, and elf could glimpse a sparkle in her eyes and the rosy softness of Grandma Elf's cheeks. Her warmth hugged elf. The same thing happened to Grandpa Elf when he would play with elf and her brother or go fishing. She was mesmerized by a charming magic when Grandpa Elf connected to nature and showed his playful spirit, which she never saw when he was with Grandma Elf.

Someone older, a supposed friend of the family, began treating elf in peculiar ways that made elf very uncomfortable. She saw him as an ogre, an eerie character that could act like a monster when he had her alone. His name was Ug. The sight of him turned little elf's stomach.

Her family insisted she be polite to him and called her rude when she wasn't. elf learned to ignore her natural sense about avoiding him.

Ug was a top-heavy troll with muscular arms and shoulders. His head protruded from his body without a neck. He was uncomfortably quiet and shy in front of adults, with a forced grin on his bulging face. She smelled a strange odor when he was around and it made her cringe.

Ug was so lonely and odd that elf's parents felt sorry for him. The giant ogre acted hopelessly shy and hid his dark side from respectable adults. elf's parents fell for a lie that this fiend made up years ago when he was kicked out of his troll community. They, too, were so lonely and ashamed of themselves. The harsh and unfair expectations placed on them from a very young age had caused them to be untrue to who they really were. They didn't understand that elves who are properly nurtured develop the ability to protect themselves and the ones they love.

Ug was very conniving and lured elf into dark places by setting out shiny toys. He violated elf by pressing his body against hers. elf was watchful of steering other youngins in a different direction to protect them from Ug. She couldn't understand how she got herself in the predicament of being with Ug, since instinctively she would do anything to protect others from his intrusions.

When elf got wise to Ug's tricks to get her alone, she avoided him, but Ug hid where he could grab her without her expecting it. The ogre touched her private parts and threatened more harm if she told anyone.

elf was so young and didn't know about sex. When she'd fight to get away he'd hurt her even more. It was horribly disturbing and scary. She no longer felt that her body was her own private property. Not only had he inappropriately touched her body, but he also wrongly blamed her. She accepted the blame, which made her think she was at fault. elf did her best to protect herself by having her mind go away, as if she disappeared. She believed she should be able to stop what he was doing to her body, but he was so much stronger.

She was afraid to tell, so she gave her mom kvetching signals. "Mommy, I don't want to be by Ug, I'm afraaaaid of him. He is soooo horribly mean!" Her head curled down as she felt herself dwindle and shrivel.

Her mom refused to listen and got mad at elf. "Go fetch some water, I am sick and tired of all your whining!" elf wanted so much for her hurting to end that at times, a part of her wanted to die.

Despite all the confusion, she could still let her imagination create interesting ways to play. She especially enjoyed playing in her grandparent's underground passage.

Once, when elf was joyfully abandoned to delightful play, she suddenly got a whiff of the troll's scent. Terrified, she ran to leave. Ug appeared from where he'd been hiding in a shadowy corner. The little elf could not make sense of what happened next. She couldn't fight the giant to get him off of her even though she struggled with all the strength she had. It hurt terribly in her private parts. She'd never before felt such excruciating pain. She screamed until her mind disappeared. No one upstairs could hear elf's desperate cries because the ogre covered her mouth. elf fought to get away, but the selfish ogre held her down.

elf finally got loose, although she had no memory of her escape, and ran to her mother and father. She blurted out what happened. Her parents did not understand her words, or didn't want to. The words sounded naughty to them.

Her parents, in denial of their own painful issues, couldn't acknowledge elf's agony. They acted numb. Her sobbing made it even harder to understand her words. Baffled and stunned by her parents' reaction, elf was too little to understand that they were in shock and could not let themselves see her trauma. elf longed for them to care for her. She felt like she didn't belong, even though they were at her grandparents' house.

elf's mother and grandmother put her to bed for a nap. When she woke up, elf felt calmer. She tried again to tell her grandmother and mother what happened. They told her it must have been a bad dream. elf cried and tried to tell them that the scary and hurtful event was something real that happened before the nap; it was not a dream!

Grandmother Elf and Mother Elf seemed too confused themselves to hear the little elf's truth. They covered their own fear with puckered brow frowns to intimidate elf. After all, the ogre was trusted by the family, and they were too embarrassed to ask him questions about this. They believed such things should not be talked about! It was easier to be in denial than to confront Ug.

Being ignored by the elves she loved the most was as painful as what had happened. She thought they loved her, but it stole her light and joy when no one cared about her pain.

She went to bed as soon as they got home. Exhausted and feeling ever so alone, she slept all night and through the morning, not waking until the sun was high in the sky. The smile on her mother's face told her that her mother was happy to see her, but Momma Elf seemed to have forgotten what had troubled elf so much. elf wanted her mommy to be happy with her. elf hid her bad memory inside herself, and with all her might she forced away reality. She could not even trust her own thoughts if her parents did not believe her story. She felt so mixed up. It was like being in a frightening, confusing maze.

The ogre never approached elf again. She could see that he avoided her. In her mind, she saw a clear image of her father confronting Ug. She sensed that her father had threatened the ogre and told him to stay away from his daughter, though her father never talked with elf about it. Even her father seemed to be hiding from the truth. He usually acted with more integrity than elf's mom, so elf trusted him more and endlessly waited for him to acknowledge her heartache.

She thought something was terribly wrong with her and was not able to relax. elf took on extra responsibility by continually looking out for Bevin and young elf neighbors. She kept them together by engaging them in games, away from dark places where the ogre may have hidden. Taking care of others helped her forget about her overwhelming confusion, but only provided temporary relief. She didn't understand that over-caretaking buried the bigger, confusing mess. elf was doing the best she could, even though she did not believe she was doing things well.

elf pasted a fake smile on her face to hide her confusion from her family and friends. She did not have words or understanding to name the abuse. It was tiring to keep the depressing trauma locked up. elf had no idea how to get help or that she needed it.

She interpreted the neglect of her truth as her being unimportant and believed that she deserved to have her name start with a small letter "e," as her mother wrote it. She didn't recognize the loneliness she felt when she was with others. She just felt awkward and different. She felt safest and most able to connect with those younger than her, for only then did she feel less vulnerable.

The little elf could still play, but she felt like something was missing. There was a deep sadness inside, but elf didn't know where the sadness was hiding. At times, elf could forget about feeling scared. As elf forgot the parts of herself that had been so hurt, the pain got pushed deeper inside her. Those befuddled, mixed up parts felt like no one in the world cared about her. She believed she did not matter and was not good enough for others to love.

When an elf's spirit shrinks, the potency of what she is really made of gets hidden inside. This little elf's inkling of her spirit was so tiny, her hope vanished. It was as if her spark was hidden inside a shell.

Was her hope lost for good? Sometimes, darkness was all elf could feel inside. She had learned from nature that life brings serendipity when it is most needed. Could she hold onto the thread of hope, anticipating that in time, despair would be turned into something better?

Chapter ~ 3 ~

Inside a Shell

To celebrate her birthday, elf's Godparents, her aunt and uncle, took her to the seashore where they were building a pixie cottage for themselves. It was a beautiful summer day, and her Godparents were fun to be with. They treated her with a special respect. At first, it felt awkward to receive such positive attention, but she liked it and grew to enjoy spending time in their presence.

They must have sensed elf's need for an adventure like this. They had tried to warm up to elf's parents, hoping they could have an honest talk about what they saw happening in the family, but Mother Elf pretended everything was fine and refused to talk about feelings. Mother Elf judged people who talked about negative events or feelings and insisted on acting positive, even if it was artificial. The best her Godparents could do was provide a comforting space for elf as they created their new cottage.

elf had begun to take nature for granted and no longer felt the special connection she knew before the ogre came and her life changed. elf felt distant, as if she were not all there. Her little nature spirit did not feel fully present to the beauty and energy that had once nourished her, but on this special day, as elf played on the beach, the ocean had a special effect on her. With the loud rush of water pouring toward her, elf started feeling more alive. Awareness emerged from the numb place inside. elf's senses began to wake up and she felt pleasure in connecting to Mother Nature again. The smell of the ocean air and the playful breeze in her hair swept her stress away like magic!

elf observed how nearby wildflowers turned to the sun to be nurtured. elf's gift allowed her to see the sun's warm rays reach to meet each plant, as if to hug and kiss the flowers like a responsive parent. elf lifted her head and arms to soak in the bright, shining sun.

Energized deep inside by the sun, elf started to tingle from the top of her head to the tips of her toes, as if every cell in her body smiled. With gratitude, she felt the love for herself, that she had once known, again growing inside her heart. Her sense that "everything was all right" returned with a deeper knowing than an elf usually gained in only seven years of living. She wondered how this renewed nature connection could unfold and bless the world.

Her senses heightened, elf stood, delighted by the diamonds in the sand sparkling at elf as she welcomed the seashells being washed up by the waves. She sensed that the shells, too, felt renewed after their long journey in the ocean. They were grateful to be acknowledged by elf and re-energized by the warm embrace of the sun.

As part of her ability to commune with nature, elf had the special gift of being able to sense what others felt. It helped her listen and care sincerely for others. She didn't yet understand that she needed to be careful to also take care of her own self.

A huge pastel shell, glistening from a spot where the grass line met the sand, caught her attention. For some reason, elf sensed a great sadness in the shell. This sense of sadness reminded elf of the sad parts still hidden inside of her and her own lonely feelings. On other days, elf would have walked the other way, but on this sun-filled, ocean play day, elf was curious.

elf ventured forward, drawn toward this unique, sparkly seashell. When elf peered into the shell's dark opening, she saw bright, sparkling eyes inside the wide crevice.

elf was surprised. She did not know that beings lived inside shells. "Whoa! Aaaaaaa... Whooooo-o are youuu?" whispered elf.

Two hazel colored eyes blinked rapidly inside the shell.

elf, a bit louder, asked again, "Who are you?"

A tiny, startled voice stuttered, "N-n-no-no-nobody?"

elf blinked and shook her head in disbelief. "You can't be nobody! You have to be somebody! You have eyes. You can see. That makes you somebody."

elf suddenly felt like an expert on BEING somebody in comparison to the voice. This voice in a seashell was obviously hiding. elf was getting ready to tell this voice off when she saw a trickle of water drip from the eyes.

She asked in a gentle voice, "Are you alright?"

A soft whimper followed, then got louder like a baby's cry. elf stepped back, scared that she had hurt the voice with the shiny eyes. elf thought of running away, but she knew this voice mattered more than the voice seemed to know.

Just then the shaky voice pleaded, "Please don't go. Don't leave me yet."

"O...kay...," responded elf. "What do you want? What do you need?"

The voice hesitated. No one had ever asked what it needed.

"How... would I know... what I need?"

Well, this question stumped elf. She thought out loud. "I... well, um, um... I don't know." elf realized that she didn't know how to know what she needed yet, either.

Then elf felt the light, tickling touch of a dragonfly on her shoulder. The touch reminded her of the sunshine tingle she felt earlier. "Sometimes," began elf, speaking out loud as she explored her awareness, "I start to breathe in the air. I imagine the freshness of the air providing me with the answer I need. Breathing like that can be magical."

elf relaxed as she followed her own advice. Actually, breathing the fresh ocean air made elf feel better. As elf continued to relax into her breathing, she pictured the very cells in her body starting to smile again. elf knew everything would be all right.

Hearing a loud, shallow breath being drawn into the shell, brought elf's awareness to the Being inside. She heard the forced breathing continue in and out, until eventually it flowed with ease. elf's inner light, so recently recharged by the glowing sun, seemed to penetrate inside the shell. It felt like elf was helping to relieve the stress the Being held inside.

The voice inside the shell sighed, "Aaaaaaahh, I really like your light. I am not used to anyone caring about me."

Just then, elf's uncle called her to come back. elf told the eyes in the shell, "I have to go. Are you going to be okay?"

"I am now," said the voice. "Can I keep the light you shared?"

"Of course. There is always more light and kindness available. And

I have more light inside me because you received it. You helped me remember I have light and hmmm... value, to share. Bye now!"

elf waved to the shell. "I will come back when I can."

As elf ran along the beach to her uncle, her feet sinking into the sand and springing up again, she laughed gleefully, aware that the hope-less shell had found hope through elf! elf felt like a miracle had taken place, first within herself and then with the "somebody" in the shell. It made the part inside elf—the part that felt she did not matter—feel noticed in some way. She felt important to someone. That part now wanted to matter, even though elf felt a bit of fear about this new desire as well.

Shifting Feelings

After her encounter with the shell on the seashore, elf kept wondering what she needed. She sensed that part in her that wanted to know she mattered. elf did a breathing exercise:

Breathe in slowly,

breathe out slowly... Aaaaahhh...

elf kept following that rhythmic pattern. She could feel herself becoming aware of her own Being.

Breathe in... feeling safe now...

And... AAAaaahhhhhhhh.

She laid down in the soft, green grass, letting her imagination flow while she watched billowy clouds shift slowly in the blue sky. As she perceived them making shapes for her, she sensed the presence of something greater than herself—something in nature that she recognized she was connected to. Receiving this caring energy reminded her how much the earth and the sky provided for her needs.

Chapter ~ 4 ~

Transparent Wings

Through her growing up years, elf did her best to compensate for the imperfections she faulted herself for. She didn't like who she was and struggled to make herself perfect, not realizing that was an impossible expectation for any elf. As her tension grew, so did her desire to make a change, though she was not clear how.

One delightful day, elf came upon a fairy-like sprite swinging on a tree swing. Transparent, glistening wings flowed behind her. Long, golden, curly hair danced in the breeze as the sprite leaned back. She cheerfully invited elf to join her on a nearby swing hanging from vines that dangled from the branch of a beechnut tree. It was as if stars twinkled from the sprite's wrinkly-eyed smile. elf, fascinated by her charisma, asked her name. In a voice that sounded like the ping of crystal, the sprite replied, "Susie Q." Susie Q flew so carefree on the swing that elf was sure her heart held the secret to joy.

elf said, "My name is elf." elf felt a kindred connection as the sprite's face brightened more. After chatting a while, elf couldn't contain her curiosity about Susie Q's happy spirit. She inquired, "What makes you so happy?"

Susie Q shared the secret way she threw her worries away while she swings. As she swung forward, she imagined her troubles flying out in front of her and continuing away, even as the swing brings her back. Swinging backward, she floated into carefree timelessness and peace. "Nothing makes me happier than swinging like this. Everything else in my day goes smoother then," Susie Q explained to the little elf.

elf gave it a try. elf felt better while she was with Susie Q, perhaps because Susie Q's energy was so light and fun. She had heard that fairies and sprites could be nature angels. elf felt she had found a personal angel in Susie Q.

After swinging with Susie Q, elf went home to do chores. As she worked, elf tried to be positive. She imagined Susie Q there beside her, talking with her. That helped elf like herself more. elf noticed how she wanted to feel about herself and held those feelings in her heart.

That night though, elf's sleep was disrupted by a nightmare that frightened her. She sobbed uncontrollably. This had happened before, but the content of the dream always escaped when she woke, except for the beginning. It would start with a male monster chasing her around the walls. Her feet touched the walls while her body was sideways, hovering parallel to the floor. Terrified, trying to escape the monster, she ran up the wall faster and faster so she would not fall.

In previous dreams she could not recall the terrible thing that happened next. She would get past the darkness by waking up, yet her energy seemed stuck inside that shadow. The horror and physical pain stayed with her. This time she remembered what happened next. A large, dark, monster-like shadow devoured her. She was completely trapped inside the frightening shadow. She couldn't comprehend the details of what she was suffering.

Waking, she shivered, feeling naked even though she wore pajamas and was bundled under blankets. Her genitals felt tense and sore. This nightmare brought back a fear that she would get hurt. It stirred memories of being hurt. She had forgotten the sexual abuse she had endured at a younger age. The dark cloud she had hidden inside seemed to be getting lighter as it released vague images of what Ug had done to her, yet confusion haunted her.

Tearfully, elf asked the Nature Spirits for help, expressing her intense need for comfort. Each teardrop was a strong plea to feel safe again. Little did she know, tears with intention are the most powerful prayer possible! Eventually, the exhausted elf fell back to sleep.

In the morning she woke with a quiet stillness, but sadness enveloped her like a shadow as she stumbled to prepare for school.

Chapter ~ 5 ~

Guardian of Undercover Treasures

Elf was amazed by the unexpected synchronicity of a response to her prayer. A gnome came to the elven school to talk with the fairies and elves. Gnomes are known for guarding underground treasures in the earth. This gnome's name was Gerome. He was a wise, stout man with a whitish beard and rather long, white hair. He had a soft look to his face with a kindhearted expression. Gerome spoke slowly and thoughtfully with a gentleness that elf could feel. The youngsters felt empowered by his conviction that they had a right to keep their bodies safe. The gnome was a sex educator, brought in to teach students about protecting their own undercover treasures.

Gerome introduced a program for prevention of sexual abuse. He knew the importance of teaching the young to value their bodies and their sexuality. He taught the class about safe touch and bad touch and their right to keep their body private. He told the class that sexual abuse was a secret no youngin should have to keep, and that keeping the secret caused many youngins to dislike themselves and feel disgust about their bodies.

elf listened very carefully. She started to recognize that the gnome was talking about the jumbled mess she experienced after her own real life trauma. The complicated mess was emerging from her subconscious. Gerome explained that the subconscious mind was hidden from one's awareness. He said, "It protects one from dealing with trauma when there is no help available. It's like trapping parts of one's self in a basement until a resolution can be created."

elf learned that what happened to her was called "sexual abuse," and that many adults had experienced this type of abuse as children and had not been able to get help. Without help, they froze emotionally and were likely to still be stuck in feeling helpless, even when they grew up. elf wondered if this was why her parents could not accept or understand when she struggled to tell them what the evil ogre had done to her.

Although elf's occasional nightmares had stirred some forgotten memories, she was troubled over not knowing what had really happened. Her feelings of disgust were jarring faint recollections of inappropriate control by the ogre. She sensed that Gerome was providing a doorway for her to reclaim her body as her sacred treasure and move toward emotional freedom.

Gerome explained that survivors of abuse experience confusion about setting boundaries and taught them that they had the right to set limits on touch. Gerome spoke gently, but with certainty. "I wish the world were safe for everyone, but there are times it is not. Some adults have not developed good judgment and behave in ways that do not respect other's boundaries. It's not always adults that take advantage of a child. Sometimes older child kin use wrong behavior with younger kin. They mistreat wee folk with inappropriate touch or by exposing private body parts. There are many ways they can cause harm to a growing youth.

"Young ones may not be able to stop a grown-up or larger being who violates their boundaries. Wee folk may not even know it is wrong for someone to do that to them. Or they may be embarrassed and unable to speak about it. Sexual abuse can make youngins freeze! These youngins often blame themselves because they didn't stop it or get away."

Gerome paused and compassionately looked around the room at all the interested elf and fairy faces. "Freezing is a response to the shock of what is happening. It makes a body unable to move, like being temporarily paralyzed. Even a part of the mind gets paralyzed. They may be too stunned to speak freely or take action, but inside they are filled with tangled thoughts and intense emotions. This is called trauma."

elf felt like Gerome was calling her to creep out of the maze of confusion and fear that haunted her dreams. Gerome made her feel safe, although she was still afraid that she did not have the words to describe what had happened to her. She feared terribly that she would say the wrong words and feel more humiliated. His calmness soothed her feelings of craziness.

"Sometimes," he continued, "a youth may try to tell someone what happened, but the one they tell may not know what action to take. He or she may not know what words to say to a youngin who has been abused. A guardian may feel helpless or frozen if they had been abused. Their mind might even deny such abuse could have occurred. Ignoring the truth is called 'being in denial.' Unless someone chooses to be open to truth, there is little we can do to change them."

elf was relieved to learn that it wasn't her fault that her parents did not talk with her when she shared her painful experience with them. A part of her needed to know they really did love her and that they were sad she had experienced such horrible hurt and shame. Even though she had more understanding of her parents' lack of compassion for her, elf longed for them to acknowledge that she had been violated and that her pain did matter.

Gerome kept talking. "Every youngin needs to know he or she is lovable and good. There are healthy adults who can teach this truth. Unfortunately, many who are now adults had not been taught that they had the right to their own bodies. They were often taught to not talk about undercover treasures, and sex was hushed up as a taboo topic. Many adults still refuse to discuss any issues around sexual misbehavior. Some parents ignore what they see happening. Some even act out inappropriate sexual conduct on their offspring and then blame the youngster! It sounds like insanity."

Gerome, the treasure guardian, soothingly said, "The truth is, when someone older does something to a youngin's private body parts, it is not the fault of the child, and the child did not do anything wrong. Never. A youth or teen is innocent and is never responsible for an older person's wrong actions or wrong touch."

As she heard those words, elf's shoulders and belly relaxed. elf sensed she could trust the gnome to be telling the truth, especially when he said that every child needs to know he or she is lovable and good.

Gerome offered to meet with anyone who needed to talk. Hesitantly, elf signed up to talk with him. At first, she was afraid to say anything, but his authentic manner eased her fear, and the secret poured out through sobs. He asked elf if she was comfortable with him contacting her parents. She gave her okay, hoping her parents would respond, but she had her doubts.

Gerome remarked on elf's courage, which helped her slowly realize how truly brave she was to try again to tell someone! She was glad that Gerome understood her heart-wrenching challenge to believe it was alright to feel.

Gerome contacted elf's parents to explain elf's need for support. Her mother sharply replied she would not talk with him or anyone about that topic. She claimed that elf had made up the stories about Ug. Nonetheless, she gave permission for elf to see him or whoever could help her, but with strict instructions that she did not want to hear any more about it. Gerome understood Mother Elf's anger and denial. He did not want to agitate her any more. Her abrupt response showed him the challenge elf would encounter as she forged ahead with her healing.

Gerome informed elf as gently as he could about his conversation with her mother. They discussed elf's right to receive help to care for herself. She shared her longing for validation from her family. elf knew she might not get it from them, so when Gerome asked if she would be willing to receive validation from others who would earn her trust, she agreed.

Gerome suggested that she allow feelings of validation to fill her by imagining validation from the Universe surrounding her. elf imagined pulling the validation into her body through all sides—front, back, right, left, above, and below. She allowed herself to embrace her truth and give her inner elf validation.

Then, Gerome asked her to practice detaching from the need for her parents' support. "Detaching is a soft form of disengaging, without extra drama. Detach by allowing them to have a different point of view than you. Create space for yourself to have a right to your own point of view. Seek support from others who can truly witness your experience."

elf shared how much her family meant to her and how difficult it would be to detach from their denial. Yet, she understood the importance of caring for herself in this way.

He explained that in the fairy realm, communities often form that act as a supportive family. These healthy, family-like communities respond to one's needs only to the degree required, with the intent of building strength within that one. elf's family was able to provide for her physical needs and some of her mental and emotional essentials, but elf also needed a spiritual exchange and more mental and emotional affirmation for her whole Self.

So, Gerome and elf envisioned a new like-minded community of helpers surrounding her, and elf knew it was a brief matter of time for that dream to manifest. She could feel their presence around her warming her. elf felt celebrated by imagining this true kinship on its way. Their gratitude for this creation made the dreaming a very powerful activity.

She had a few more meetings with Gerome. Although her trust grew, a part of her also grew very suspicious since he was a male. Her memories of the sexual abuse were becoming clearer, yet elf struggled with her inability to voice her trauma.

At times, Gerome misunderstood her, and she felt absolutely devastated. She thought he was dismissing her suffering. She wasn't aware that this thought surfaced from emotions stuck by the trauma of her parents' denial. A part of elf was afraid that Gerome would not believe her either. Sometimes she felt so muddled and fearful, she didn't know whether the sexual assaults had really happened with the ogre or not. The more elf tried to convince herself they had not happened, the more she would cry uncontrollably.

Gerome sincerely apologized, saying he did not want her to feel dismissed again. He said he understood how talking about this situation touched on a tender topic for elf, and he wanted to help her recover from the abuse as well as from the ordeal with her parents.

Gerome recommended that elf see a female fairapist. He explained; "Talking with the fairapist will help you be compassionate with yourself and recognize the truth in you. It is not healthy to ignore pain inside. Everybody deserves to be treated fairly and to have the opportunity to heal the hurt that comes from being dishonored."

Then, Gerome told elf about a caring and sensitive fairapist who specializes in recovery from childhood trauma, including sexual abuse. elf felt relieved that Gerome suggested a female to share her most terrifying secrets with, and she felt more secure that there was a plan to help her. She could feel her body relax, because she knew Gerome wanted to respect her most personal feelings. The wise gnome also encouraged elf to have fun and relax when she could.

Gerome helped her feel confident in reasoning through what was right for her. He suggested elf let him know when she felt ready to meet Fae, the fairapist. elf liked that these decisions were her choice.

He told elf, "You are the one who will decide if you are comfortable with Fae or not. You will know if someone is helpful in your quest to find peace of mind. These consultations can be very personal and are meant to be a comfort to you as you sort out what is troubling. If this fairapist does not feel right for you, she and I will help find a healing fairy who is. She will not take it personally; her job is to support what you need."

To help elf mentally prepare for her first appointment, the caring gnome described the healing fairy's treehouse studio. elf was apprehensive about sharing the private layers of her emotional unrest, yet she clung to the hope that someone could help.

elf returned home mindful of her growing ability to be more mature than her parents. She asked her Source, the Creator of all life, to bring forgiveness through her, while at the same time guiding her to detach from them in a wise way. Her journal was filled with grief and reasons to create distance from her mother. She had often tussled with ways to love her mother or get her approval, and now recognized that it was herself that elf needed to put first. elf sketched all kinds of reminders in her journal with drawings for her intention. She learned that as she grew stronger, her mother might disapprove of her even more.

elf learned to recognize the hurt little elf child in her mother, and chose to surround her mother with love and light. When she needed it, elf could call on Susie Q and Gerome to help envision her mother in light and love.

Over time, Mother Elf seemed to soften and show more kindness and new understanding, but she still had many limitations. Because Mother Elf was not interested in personal growth and confined herself to what was comfortable for her, elf knew she could not trust that her mother would hear her heart.

elf found more comfort in communicating with nature, which opened her heart to receive all that was safe and good for her. Gratitude for these blessings brought her serendipitous gifts that continued to multiply as gratitude grew.

Chapter ~ 6 ~

Treasured Friendship

elf played a lot with Susie Q because she was kind and made elf laugh. elf so enjoyed being with the lively sprite that she imagined Susie Q never had any serious problems. Susie Q seemed so comfortable and caring.

One day, Susie Q told elf that she did not feel like herself. She had told her mom something, and her mom had not believed her. Susie Q cried, "It makes me think she does not trust me… and that makes a part of me want to give up! I've worked so hard to learn to trust myself again!"

elf could not believe she was hearing Susie Q say words that elf thought only she hid inside. elf asked, "What do you mean? You worked so hard?"

"Well, I have," said the squelched sprite with a long sigh. "I have a fairapist who helps me see clearly. A long time ago, my world was turned upside down by something called incest."

Stunned by the disclosure, elf stared wide-eyed at her friend. Was Susie Q really telling her that she had been sexually abused by a relative? elf remembered Gerome talking about incest, which is an inappropriate sexual behavior that can include any touching—by a family member—of another family member's private parts, or making a relative touch his or her private parts. Whichever family member it is done to—whether it is a daughter, son, grandchild, sister, brother, niece, or nephew—it is incest, it is morally wrong, and it is against the law for an adult to do this. It can cause the victim, which means someone who was taken advantage of, a lot of physical, mental, and emotional harm, and often results in the victim disconnecting from her or his unique spirit.

For Susie Q, the abuse did not stop until she told her fairapist about it. Even though Susie Q was now safe from the abusive behavior, she still got scared at times, and her old awful feelings and mind-muddles still were triggered.

"I am so sorry, elf!" Susie Q said. "I didn't mean to go on about me and all this stuff. It is just that you are such a good listener, and you seem to understand me."

"Ooooh, I guess… I… I mean, I do… understand most of it," stuttered elf. "I must have been abused, too, because I wake up from nightmares of someone touching my undercover treasures and my body hurts. I feel both angry and excited, which makes me feel all mixed up. I get so unsure of myself that I question if it really happened. I never imagined that it happened to you, too. You seem so happy and carefree!"

"I have been happy a lot more lately," admitted Susie Q. Fairy dust appeared out of nowhere as she expressed gratitude, so she sprinkled it over the two of them. "My fairapist and my Safe Peeps have helped me SOOO MUCH!"

elf's head tingled and the sensation moved down her body as the magic dust settled on her and lightened her spirit. She smiled with joy upon witnessing the same flow as Susie Q moved through pain to a lighter state of being.

Susie Q took a deep breath and out came a loud exhale, as if it released her troubles. She shared how she felt safe and really cared for now that she worked with her fairapist. elf asked a lot of questions and suddenly couldn't wait to meet the fairapist that Gerome had in mind for her.

elf also loved hearing about the sprite's Safe Peeps. "They are other people I can confide in," explained Susie Q. "Safe Peeps promise to respect you without judging you. They promise to do their best to understand you by accepting your feelings and experiences."

"You don't want to go blurting what happened to you to just anyone," Susie Q warned elf, as if she had learned that lesson the hard way. She explained, "Not everyone has experienced this abuse, and they may not understand. I have felt awkward and even hurt when someone else does not comprehend the suffering I experienced. For now, it feels safer to be discreet by sharing only with those who could understand or help me. Perhaps in the future, I could learn to inform others of the empathy and understanding that could be offered to a survivor. At this time, I take their view or misunderstanding too personally."

"What do you mean by a survivor?" asked elf, furling her brow.

"A survivor can refer to someone who makes efforts onward in life after going through a tremendous challenge. Sometimes it relates to someone who fought a deadly illness or escaped death in some way. In our case, it relates to the strength it takes to endure the craziness of having been sexually abused and still forge ahead to live," responded Susie Q.

Susie Q asked elf if she would be a Safe Peep for her, but elf told Susie Q that she didn't think she would be very good at helping her.

"Oh, elf, you are a big help. You're such a great listener, and you also help by sharing your own truth," Susie Q exclaimed, reaching out to offer elf a gentle hug.

elf was amazed that she could feel so good about helping someone who had gone through a trauma similar to what elf wished had never happened. elf took a deep breath and allowed the good emotions to wash over her.

It delighted elf that she and Susie Q would now be Safe Peeps for one another. They said their good-byes, acknowledging an intent to keep each other in their heart. elf meandered home with a toasty feeling that she had special gifts and they were beginning to bud!

On her way home, elf remembered the "mystery Being " in the shell on the beach. elf wished that the "Being" could feel hopeful like elf was starting to feel. elf imagined the light washing over and inside the shell, once again touching the little one who peered out of the seashell. She sensed their connection spanning the distance and it inspired her.

Chapter ~ 7 ~

Meeting the Fairapist

Gerome was able to schedule elf to meet the fairapist in a few days. When the day came, elf waited with Gerome in the fairapist's waiting room, feeling both eager and nervous. Her knees felt wobbly when she walked in, but the sight of cascading branches outside of the fairapy studio calmed her.

The fairapy studio was located high up in the hollow area of a weeping willow tree. elf breathed deeply, sensing the warmth and strength of the tree spirit. The room had striking views of wispy branches beholding fresh, delicate leaves. Something about the fluid curves of the weeping willow helped elf's tense body soften. Looking out, elf sensed she was about to understand a broader perspective of a grand world.

Gerome introduced a tall, flowing fairy named Fae. She had golden-silver hair that changed shades depending on how it shimmered in the light. The graceful fairapist greeted elf with a warm smile, and elf relaxed more. Fae did her best to reach elf's heart with the light that generated from deep within her heart. That light pulsed through her iridescent wings when she met someone who desired personal growth. Fae could see an expressive spirit hiding inside this timid, worried, little body and indeed more light radiated from Fae in this meeting.

elf became even more comfy when the three of them sat and visited. Gerome suggested he leave if elf was content, and she nodded approvingly with a smile. Fae gave elf her full attention. Feeling affirmed and understood, elf shyly expressed her gratitude for being warmly accepted.

elf learned that when one is violated at a young age, the victim often loses a sense of acceptance and positive self-worth. Validation by someone who believes in the survivor helps restore one's sense of self and value. Elf was amazed that already her body was beginning to feel lighter as an inner confidence seemed to smile inside.

Self-Care for Trauma or Overwhelming Fear

Fae compassionately explained she wanted elf to feel safe. She gave elf a list of some positive and caring things elf could do for herself if fear seemed to take over. "Keep this reminder handy and refer to it when you need to feel safe." Then Fae read the list to elf. The first item suggested that if elf ever gets panicked, she can bring herself back to the present by asking herself today's date and reminding herself that the abuse is over.

Fae expounded, "When past trauma is triggered, it comes from a part of you that has been frozen in time. Your emotions from childhood trauma are attached to a younger age. They are encoded in the brain and triggered when memories of that time are released. You can free past emotions by telling your inner child your current age, slowing your breathing, and reassuring your inner child you are now safe."

Fae continued to read, "Take time to allow your body to relax, much like caring for a baby or younger elf that is hurt and crying.

Patiently speak calming words to your wounded part; this needs to be sustained longer than the fear and upset. It requires endurance and kindness, but when you stick with it, your inner child eventually learns to trust you." She added, "These are important first steps. We will be following up with ways to free your inner child." Then, Fae invited her to come back in a few days.

elf was over the moon about meeting Fae and having another really Safe Peep in her life. When she walked out of Fae's office, elf's knees felt stable, her body flowed with great ease, and her stomach was calm. She noticed the sun dancing with the shade from the leaves as the breeze gently bounced branches around. All of her senses were enlivened as she strolled with renewed hope.

The next day, Gerome checked to inquire about elf's comfort level with the fairapist. elf explained, "Fae was such a good listener. Talking made me feel better. Fae's eyes held so much empathy and caring for the scared parts of me, that I felt safe. I want to express myself more and hear what she has to say."

elf continued to see Fae for fairapy once a week. The experience was rewarding, and yet it was an uneasy struggle through some stretches. In working through the toughest issues, elf got the most relief and sense of freedom. At times, she cried with embarrassment, contemptuously referring to herself as acting like a baby.

Fae shared that in truth, elf was very brave. Fae reminded her that when one is abused, the young part who was harmed remains trapped back in the time when the abuse happened. For elf, that young part was still reacting out of the emotion that was frozen when she was abused.

Connecting with utmost empathy, Fae reassured elf, "Your inner child needs to be tended to in order to recover. You are assisting her by allowing her to express her hurt and let her tears be seen. You are helping her by giving the pain a voice. This not only releases the pain; it also renews your strength. The ache lessens as you let it out."

Fae sincerely and respectfully expressed that she admires the courage it takes for someone to seek help with recovery from very painful memories. elf sensed her mind opening to renewed consideration as she assimilated Fae's view of her and then followed as Fae guided her to care for the distressed part of herself. What an uplifting experience for her inner child to feel absolutely precious to Fae and to herself!

As elf opened up about what the ogre had done to her, she felt strength and certainty in her body. Her confusion and fear shrunk as her fairapist intently listened to what had happened in these terrifying encounters. The sense of a bigger Self allowed elf to begin surrendering her sorrow and pain. The change felt like a miracle, but she had so much more to release and take care of before she could speak about this strong Self.

In the sessions to follow, feeling complete safety when held by Fae's mystical eyes, elf could not hold back the truth of her past; it flowed as she let the words and emotion pour out of her. She discovered an inner power by expressing the painful memories she had been trained to repress. Relief transformed her spirit and freed her inner child when she saw belief and understanding conveyed in Fae's eyes.

elf's kindness toward herself increased by opening to receive compassion and encouragement to be real! Indeed, this was a magical gift with a dual purpose. Not only could elf receive Fae's tenderhearted help, she could also tenderheartedly witness her own agony, accept validation, and attend to her personal needs.

The delicate gold rims enhancing Fae's large wings began to flutter as she observed elf's goodwill expanding toward herself. It gave Fae a positive energy flow to witness healing grace cascade upon those she attended to. Fae knew that when trauma victims experienced this empathy and care for themselves, their path began to align with the higher good they deserved in their life. Fae's wings continued to quiver with delight as she witnessed elf realizing this joyful process.

To progress in recovery, elf needed to seek empathy. Where could she get it? All she had known was her family's multilayered neglect and denial of the abuse. She longed to have others respond with care when she felt hurt. As she experienced a caring response from others like Fae, she was able to start responding with care to the shame and upset inside of her.

A Safe Container ~ to Emote in a Constructive Way

Fae had taught elf the importance of expressing herself when she needed. At the end of a session, elf told Fae, "I'm worried about not being able to share my strong feelings with my mom or dad."

Fae gave elf a journal in which to write her emotions. elf gently caressed the fragrant paper, which was made from recycled paper and flower petals. It had been handmade by a previous group of survivor-thrivers who wanted to pass a gift on to a survivor starting the healing journey. "This can be your safe container for feelings and personal thoughts," Fae declared.

elf liked the idea of having a container to empty her secret feelings into. She felt hopeful, knowing that others who had been in the painful place she was in, had gotten stronger. The journal would continue to remind her of that.

elf was grateful that Fae also encouraged her to imagine things she enjoyed. "Feel free to write about any small pleasure! Your enjoyment is the reward and the reason for facing this challenge."

elf relished the bond she felt with Fae and the ideas that helped her feel good about herself. She was learning to emote in a safe way. As recreation filled more of her time, it became natural for her to feel more joy. Having fun balanced the inside work elf had done in fairapy with the occasional grim writing or drawings she kept in her journal.

As elf grew emotionally, she started making new friends and revived forgotten interests. One of her favorite re-discovered loves involved leisurely exploring beautiful flowers and filling her being with their fragrance.

Imagine how huge a flower head is to a pocket-sized elf. Sometimes, a fairy invited her inside a blossom. She would carefully slip in, feel the energy, and allow herself to be held tenderly by delicate, silky petals. A rest or nap inside that soft nest rejuvenated her.

One bright, starry night, elf wrote in her journal:

> "My healing journey has led me such a long way already. I notice as I change, that I am finding more thoughts and feelings to enjoy. When I can enjoy the sweetness of life, my uncomfortable memories fade. Still, I cannot ignore the discomfort of shame and hidden emotions. Now I know there is a time for all of my feelings."

Love welled up deep in her chest as she basked in feelings of security. The comforting warmth of benevolence expanded throughout her body. A smile was on her lips as she dozed off to a sweet night's sleep.

Chapter ~ 8 ~

Melting the Trauma

Elf took a break from fairapy. She wanted her recovery work to be over! She tried to tell herself that her healing process was finished.

It was a challenge to enjoy herself on the outside and then switch back to attending to feelings that hurt inside. Without realizing she was doing it, elf began to deny her painful emotions, even though her previous intention had been to honor all of her feelings. Immersed in the fantasy that she had finished healing, elf was unaware of the gnawing nudges growing within that needed tending to.

A dreary, rainy day several months later stirred up elf's buried emotions. Frantic, she burst into the waiting room of Fae's treehouse office. A quick, little leprechaun fairapy assistant was the only one in that room. In elf's panic, she had made up thoughts that her fairapist and others were betraying her. The fairapy leprechaun, Lenny, calmed her in the playful way that only muses can.

When elf found out that Fae was not available to see her that day, she felt like she was going to crawl out of her skin if she didn't do something immediately! Lenny recognized the extremely impulsive behavior caused by panic.

The engaging little fairapy assistant asked what could help her feel peace. elf crinkled her whole face and scowled, not trusting that the leprechaun in front of her could help. Caught in her post-trauma frenzy, she felt trapped and powerless to get away.

Lenny politely offered, "I know an exercise that may help. It's up to you, if you want to hear it. It is your choice."

elf reflected and realized this charming leprechaun was sincere in his caring and giving her a choice. "Yesss... tell me more," she requested as her suspicions started to subside and her gut stopped burning.

Exercise to Calm the Panic

Lenny nodded and began speaking in a caring tone, "This Pendulation exercise works like magic, in a way, to shrink fear that has taken over. It will allow you to reason with the fear, in due time, without feeling threatened by it. When you recognize that the fright is coming from the past, find something with meaning to focus on so you can relax for even a few minutes. Then when you feel calm, slowly allow your mind to briefly return to the feelings of panic, and again, gently nudge yourself back to the tranquil feelings of the focal point you chose. Repeat this for ten minutes or as long as it seems to help. Gradually, the focal point will help stillness grow and will help you regain your power over the trauma reaction." (Levine, 2003)

elf's stress was so intense that she felt desperate, willing to try anything. Before starting the exercise, elf self-consciously blurted out, "While you were talking, my eyes were on the golden-white crystal sitting on the window sill. It calmed me and eased my terror a wee bit."

Lenny offered to lend the crystal to elf so she could practice the exercise. elf accepted his offer. Holding the heavy, sparkling crystal, which was twice the size of her palms, sent a warm tingling sensation through her fingers and up toward her elbows as she slipped into greater stillness.

Focused on her goal to relax, elf wanted to experiment with the exercise taught by the earnest leprechaun. A ray of hope stirred in her when the sun appeared from behind the clouds. She bid him farewell and left the wide, weeping willow tree as a light sprinkle of raindrops glistened in the sunlight.

elf's inclinations took her to a clearing in the woods. She mused at the sight of a rainbow above and the twist of fate that led to meeting the leprechaun. She delighted in watching elated weather-fairies gliding down the colored light slide in the sky. They seemed to be sharing whispers of gladness that elf could see the spectral passage.

elf sat on a baby mushroom near a creek. She let out a loud sigh as her tension softened. The trickling, bubbly sounds of the brook helped her release the hardness in her shoulders. She placed the crystal in her lap and smiled as she took in its energy. Soon, her very cells felt as though they were smiling with serenity.

The fairy realm is extremely sensitive to sensing the subtle energy in rocks, whereas many humans need to focus their imagination to attune to energies. elf basked in the calmness until she felt safe enough to experiment. Remembering what Lenny suggested, she then guided herself to revisit, as lightly as possible, her feelings of terror. She was surprised how fast they returned and how strong they were. Eventually, focusing on the crystal helped her return to feeling the smile inside.

She let out a loud audible, "Aaaaaaaahhh!" Droplets formed in her eyes, but she couldn't recognize her emotions. Thoughts of regret and shame for having so much emotion crept in as her feelings of fear returned and expanded into hopelessness.

She was now in her early teens and wanted her recovery work to be over! Returning her attention to the crystal, she sensed every cell in her body reverberating with hope. A knowing grin came over her at the synchronistic parallel of her trauma and the crystal energy to the rain showers and the sunbeams around her. As she wished to see the meaning in her experience that reflected the rainbow, she realized HOPE was her colorful, kaleidoscopic bridge. The rain, as well as the storm inside, would dissipate as she practiced swinging between the opposite emotions.

Very cautiously, elf searched again for stormy waters inside. Another swing to the other side brought up a fear of being controlled. She rode it like a huge wave, not knowing for a minute if she could return from such an intense feeling. She inhaled and stared at the rock, but it brought nothing. She felt more of the void with her exhale. Then, there was a moment of total stillness. elf followed the calm stillness and suddenly realized she could choose!

Miraculously, she felt even stronger than the rock! She could choose to feel stronger than the fear that for now melted into nothing. She felt like her body was growing instantly in size! Her sight became crystal clear! Colors and details seemed more vivid!

The shadow had shriveled. This was so much better than the panic that had shadowed her. She knew she could make it until her next visit with Fae, even though she was concerned that the unexpected, overwhelming feelings could come back in the future. She wanted to get the support needed to build her strength to face any other panic that had been buried inside.

When she got up to go home, Lenny appeared, as if out of nowhere. This jolly leprechaun showed up on her path to check that she was all right. She noticed this light-hearted character had incredible awareness and timing to be of service. She had wondered if someone who was vibrating that much joy could really care as much as he seemed to.

elf expressed her great relief from overcoming the feelings of panic. She asked if it was the crystal that had made her strong. She marveled about the solid and extraordinary energy in the rock and how at the end, she felt the magic was within her.

"How did it get inside me?" she asked.

Lenny responded, "Your power was hidden inside you. By resonating or allowing yourself to feel the vibration of the crystal, you were able to access the energy inside yourself. Your body recalled the memory as a felt-sense, like a sensation that was hidden. The abundant energy of well-being was always stored in your cells, waiting to be awakened."

This answer stunned the elf. Her eyes widened with some disbelief that this treasure was inside of her. elf liked the idea and hoped it was true. Her body relaxed with the idea, recognizing it as truth for her.

The very genuine, petite fella was gone as quickly as he said goodbye. She wished she had thanked him. After all, he helped her find a sort of magic that she would not have otherwise known how to access in her time of need.

When elf got home, she wrote a note to give Lenny when she returned the crystal. She felt a warm gratitude growing, which she did not usually feel toward males. The newness of this was exciting, yet she remembered that she couldn't yet trust her teeter-totter feelings when it came to males.

Chapter ~ 9 ~

Inner Repairs

elf showed up for her next appointment with Fae, feeling nervous and embarrassed. Fae's warm nature helped elf lighten up. elf muttered an apology for feeling angry with Fae days earlier. She was afraid that Fae would be upset with her. The fairapist's calm reaction surprised elf. Fae assured her that she was always open to hearing elf's feelings toward her, especially anger.

"I want you to feel safe expressing all of your feelings," said Fae.

elf was surprised that her intense emotions could be accepted by someone close to her. Her family did not allow her to show anger; she was punished when she spoke up. Her parents taught her to hide anger, which made her feel worse inside.

elf cautiously discussed this with Fae. "I think that something is wrong with me when I am annoyed, or even worse, when I feel angry."

Fae reassured elf that it was healthy to express and release these feelings. This allowed elf to unload the heavy shame and fear she carried. "A part of me believes that if I trust others, they'll betray me. Yet, I desperately long to trust someone. I long for connection, but I'm also afraid of it."

Fae understood and validated each and every feeling. Fae explained that her feelings were natural results of betrayals by the ogre and the adults in her family.

They sat in quiet as elf's inner awareness expanded. Suddenly, elf recalled how scared she had been days before when Fae was not accessible for her. elf blurted out the emotion that came bubbling up. "I was afraid you wouldn't be able to help me when I needed you most. I was scared that… that… " Choking back tears, she finished her sentence in a whisper, "that I was not important to you." elf feared she had said something wrong by speaking so honestly. Anticipating rejection, her body felt hot with a surge of energy. She was ready to run away.

Fae moved to the edge of her seat and put her hand on her own heart. She spoke empathically, "You are an important Being, and you mean a lot to me, elf." She held a long pause so elf could take in her truth before she proceeded. "You are right that I cannot always help you, even when you may need it most. I fully trust that you are resourceful and can seek what you need to find help."

Sitting in extended stillness, great insight dawned. elf realized it was herself who sought the help she received from Lenny and the crystal. Fae had given elf full credit for the attributes, such as seeking answers, that elf had not recognized in herself. She could tell that Fae was telling her the truth. The naming of her characteristics empowered elf, as if by magic, to trust herself to get her needs met, even if that included getting help from unexpected places. An internal vibration rose as she generated love for herself and love for her life.

elf took a deep breath and released an expressive sigh,

"Ooooooooooohh, you do have a way of relieving me of some heavy stuff, you know."

"That is because you are so willing, aware, and actively searching for truth and healing. You deserve most of the credit for your tough work," responded Fae.

Fae wisely allowed a time of stillness for elf to absorb that she was the one doing the deep healing work. elf felt suspended in time, as though her spirit, mind, emotions, and body were being downloaded like a supercomputer with an incredible update so she could function more efficiently. This new state of being was more aligned with the true nature of who she was meant to be.

In future sessions, elf courageously spoke about her occasional fear of trusting Fae. elf said she felt guilty for feeling suspicious, because Fae had been considerate and reliable.

"There is nothing wrong with your feelings," explained Fae. "Trust is something that is earned. Know that I am not perfect; I do make mistakes. I am interested in learning how I can assist your growth and wellbeing. We can work things out as I listen to your feelings and give you the respect you deserve. I want you to honor the wisdom in what you feel and sense. Do not feel obligated to trust anyone. May I suggest that you take small steps, as in baby steps, in extending your trust?"

This was completely the opposite of elf's belief that she had to extend trust to others even when it did not feel right for her. Her parents' denial left her feeling uncertain of herself and obligated to rely on an "authority". elf was relieved to have permission to extend trust in tiny increments. She responded confidently with a "yes" and a bright smile. Her guilt melted away as she embraced feeling empowered to determine the amount of trust that felt right for her.

Fae encouraged her more with a suggestion from Access Consciousness, "Listen to your sense of what feels light. It will guide you to be your best authority." elf relished the idea of being her own "best authority" and staying curious to find what felt light for her.

Chapter ~ 10 ~

Accessing Creativity and Logic

In the spring, Fae invited elf to an on-going gathering of Safe Peeps who were all recovering from abuse. The group offered members a safe space to gather and engage in exploration of self-care by increasing body awareness, self-worth, and boundaries. elf looked forward to the healing activities, facilitated by animals and insects, that would uncover her healthy instincts, which had been silenced by the abuse.

To demonstrate wholeness, the critters present shared their energy and the lessons they had learned while setting their own natural boundaries. These demonstrations helped the participants discover, through modeling and interaction, what they needed to do to develop a stronger sense of their full Selves.

Wherever the Safe Peep meetings were held, the group would form a fairy ring in a circle that was formed by nature, such as a circle of mushrooms or trees. This would be their sacred space for that meeting.

elf got to meet other girl and boy sprites, fairies, and elves who were all mending from some form of sexual abuse. Some of them were extremely sad and negative toward life, which made elf appreciate the joy she was able to feel much of the time. She recognized how much progress she had made, and that helped her feel hopeful for the ones who displayed sorrow or hopelessness. As Fae would say, "There is always hope!"

The healing group bonded while doing art and also relished the invitation to color their feelings. Afterward, they shared their very personal inner thoughts as they showed their artwork. elf was inspired by everyone's courage to share at such a delicate level, and felt a deep connection as she witnessed each individual's desire to go on in life, despite the confusion and emotional scars they carried from early abuse. At one gathering, a couple of fairies commented that expressing feelings through art helped them get in touch with and accept their emotions as a healthy part of their true Self.

Fae explained that as a result of trauma, the brain constricts the language part of the brain, therefore mapping the trauma in the right (creative) brain and also in the body. She said, "It is only through creative play accompanied by factual information that one can piece it all together—through the use of both the left and right brain! That means engaging the mental side and the imaginative feeling side of the brain, in order to help reorganize and understand what has happened. Communicating about abusive events is often necessary for that full process to take place. This is very complex, but I hope to make it easier to understand."

Fae paused to give them time to absorb this information, and then continued, "If abuse occurred before a child understands what sex is, the event is foreign—without a connection to any language or understanding of it. The memory seems lost, stored in the unconscious without a "computer icon" for it. This situation can create even more confusion unless the child receives education to help establish an inner sense of security. Art and moving the body with the intention of releasing and healing can bring feelings of safety. This leads to discovering what else is needed to restore stability."

Everyone received a leaflet from Fae which explained in simpler detail how to use each side of the brain. This is what it said:

Using Your Left Brain and Right Brain for Trauma Relief

It is important to switch back and forth between the left and right side of the brain. Balancing access to each side of the brain is a helpful skill. The more fun you have with it, the more fruitful your experience will be. Temporarily, there may be times that you may not clearly access both sides. One side may be more beneficial to help you self-soothe during trying times. Self-soothing then becomes the priority. Which side—intellectual or creative—tends to bring the most relief for you?

Accessing Left Brain Traits

The left side of the brain is the accurate, intellectual, factual, precise, and mental half of the brain. Doing activities like math, analyzing, and organizing can exercise your intellect and develop rational thinking. Play with ways you can make this left brain work rewarding for you. Here are some helpful pointers when you have difficulty thinking clearly:

1. *Ask someone you trust to help you, to ensure that you use common sense in making wise choices.*

2. *Breathe, allowing room for change as you open up to new awareness. Confusion is natural when you get a glimpse of old patterns that are not working. It is a sign that old ideas or beliefs are breaking up, letting in the*

light. Remind yourself that the confusion is temporary. It may seem like jumbled chaos or a thick fog, but when light clears the haze, visibility becomes better.

3. Slow down your busy activities and get extra rest and sleep at these times. Exercise in ways that you enjoy.

4. Keep a written account of what worked for you when your mind was muddled. Offer yourself the best self-care by referring to this as a reminder when you need it.

5. Detach from a situation, when you are having a strong emotional reaction, by approaching the problem as if you were solving a math equation, even if math tends to challenge you. Write the steps you could take to reduce your emotions and handle the problem.

6. Make a list of what you enjoy. Pick something from this list to reward yourself for simply doing your best through the most trying times of recovery. You deserve to treat yourself for work well done.

Using Your Right Brain for Relief

The right side of the brain is the creative, flowing, feeling, imaginative, and intuitive portion of the brain. Give yourself credit for opening up to your emotions. Buried emotions and memories can still come forth, even when words cannot be accessed. Acknowledging feelings helps free the real you. It is important to set up a safe space to allow the feeling side of the brain to express through activities such as:

1. Artistic expression—any type. It is the process that matters, not the end result. It's a good way to access emotions and get to know them. Here are some mediums to experiment with.

- ❖ *Play on paper with pencil, pen, crayons, or any writing tool.*

- ❖ *Apply paint to paper or canvas to match what you feel inside.*

- ❖ *Impress your feelings into clay and create a safe environment to throw the piece on the ground as a form of release.*

After you've released tension with whichever outlet you've chosen, play with ways to transform the piece of art or create a new form that expresses or holds a ritual experience of the feelings you desire. It is important to accept your artwork and not to critique it. For classes on this type of method, research Process Art.

2. Role play. Expand your perception by acting out an experience. Ask others to act out conversations that have taken place that troubled you. Observe someone acting out your role. Or, if you act it out alone, set up two or more chairs or positions and change places as you act out each character involved. First, act out something that triggers your painful emotions. Have compassion for yourself and connect to an awareness beyond the emotions. Next, act out what you wish would take place if you could do it over. Explore making different choices, having better boundaries or self-care, detaching from the other's reaction or using different words.

Remember, we cannot control another. The best we can hope for is to be a positive influence, which is powerful and makes a difference! Refrain from expecting others to accept what we offer, even if we see it as positive.

3. *Movement.* Increase awareness of sensing your physical sensations by learning body movement, such as free dance, Nia Technique®, Hanna Somatics®, also known as Somatic Movement, JourneyDance™, Yoga, or Trauma-Sensitive Yoga.

4. *Energy work (also known as body work).* There are body work modalities including: Reiki (a Japanese word meaning soul—life energy transferred by a light laying on of hands); Healing Touch (another hands-on technique that also balances the body, mind, spirit, and emotions); and Access Bars (holds 32 points on the head, allowing you to become more present and clear).

5. *Meditation; hypnosis; and tracking your dreams.* There are meditation and hypnosis recordings or classes to take you step-by-step. Some therapists and professionals are trained in dream analysis. You can try one of these practices or all if they interest you.

6. *Automatic writing.* This is a form of journaling in which you allow free-flowing ideas and feelings without thinking or analyzing them. Start by setting a timer for a minute and write whatever words come. You can add another minute for each interval you sit down to write. You could read it over and complete the exercise by writing what you desire for yourself. Enhance the energy by generating gratitude for receiving as if you have already received. The first part is cleansing and the second part builds your imagination for a better future.

Using Creativity and Logic

1. Practice patience if you have a habit of acting or speaking impulsively. Give yourself time to detach from

upset or fear. Take time to connect with nature or your heart center. Give yourself time to process by journaling about the issue and getting a full night's sleep. This will help you resolve it later. Best decisions are made from a relaxed state of mind.

2. Engage in activities that bring you the most joy. If there are certain folks or animals who are a delight to share time with, plan for that. Keep track of what brings you joy so you can remind yourself during times of stress how you can lighten up and find balance.

3. Take time to be grateful. Gratitude can be shown through art, writing, reflecting, or verbally sharing thanks for all the good things you cherish. A practice called Access Consciousness teaches that you cannot be judgmental when you are in a state of gratitude. Every day "gift" yourself with 3 to 5 things you can appreciate about yourself. This builds your confidence and feelings of well-being!

USING YOUR LEFT AND RIGHT BRAIN—SUMMARY

Since trauma constricts the language area—the left portion of the brain—the trauma is recorded in the right brain and also in the body. It is through right brain activities and associated logical work (the left side of the brain) that one can piece together recovery on every level! Using both left brain and right brain exercises, you will access and retrieve more of your true state of being.

Pay attention to your feelings and the physical sensations in your body as you create your art and explore other expressive endeavors. Sometimes the physical sensations contain messages about the abuse and where it was stored in your body. This allows you to have awareness of where trauma is contained in your body and gives you physical clues to help you release it. Most important, approach this work with a sense of lightness! Play with enjoying this new awareness or get help from someone who may be able to help you lighten up.

If you feel overwhelmed or flooded with emotions, you may want to seek help to lessen the overload. It helps when a safe person witnesses you expressing your feelings so that you will treat them fairly. When sensitive emotions have been cared for, your spirit is free, and your mind can provide clear thinking. Be considerate of your feelings and awareness, they provide information that can be used to make wise, healthy choices.

Fae informed the group that next time they would have a guest to teach them a practice that will help them learn inner communication with their bodies. Curious, some of the elves tried to guess who it could be, but Fae kept it a secret. They were all intrigued!

Chapter ~ 11 ~

Transformation...The Art of Meditation

A sweet, yellow, white, and black striped caterpillar named Ria was introduced at Fae's next gathering. Ria was the guest leader Fae had invited to lead the group for this meeting. Ria was intentional yet thoughtful as she introduced the idea of meditation for the pre-teens and teens who had been mistreated. Her patience and gentleness, which held a special magnetism, calmed their anxiety and taught them to concentrate.

Ria floated just above the group on a weeping willow tree branch that almost swayed hypnotically. She gently directed them to take a few deep breaths. "Focus on your inhale, expanding your belly and chest as you go inward. Pause—and then allow your exhale to release any thoughts or feelings you want to let go of."

The participants exhaled with loud sighs of relief. Some of them were hesitant to close their eyes, but Ria understood their fear and waited until they were ready. Soon they surrendered to the weight of their increasingly heavy lids. She brought everyone's focus to single-mindedness, reassuring the group that they would not miss anything by freeing any thoughts rushing through their minds. That helped the group slow down their racing thoughts. When relaxed, they were free to trust themselves to flow with Ria's suggestions.

Ria began with a period of silence to allow peaceful feelings to fill them. She asked them to discover the spark of light inside themselves, no matter how small it may be. "You all have a sparkle within you."

She led them through the next steps in a tone just louder than a whisper, drawing each word out longer than usual, "Use your inhale to allow the light inside you to expand. Invite the light to multiply with each breath. The light is now filling every cell in your body. It streams down the core of your body, through your legs, into your feet, and beyond your toes. The brightness moves up your trunk, through your arms, filling your hands and fingers. A beam shines up your neck and illuminates your head and mind. Now envision this radiance surrounding your entire body."

Gradually, Ria guided everyone to imagine a protective insulation forming around his or her body. She suggested choosing either a cocoon, a chrysalis, an egg shell, or a bubble to encase their body.

To elf, imagining silky, soothing strands weaving a web around her whole body made her feel so comforted that no other boundary was required. It was a cocoon of light holding space for the warm fuzzy, yet potent energy of her inner spark.

Everyone became more relaxed and calmer as they imagined forming their own natural protective field. In this tranquil, nurturing space, not only the group, but also the entire forest felt calmness settle in.

"This invisible sheath will always be available to surround and shield you in a subtle, yet profound way, because you have the power to create a sheltering bubble of any form around yourself every day, just as we have done today. You can also imagine the bubble around you in any future situation."

Before she brought the group back to awareness of their body, Ria gave them the opportunity to envision daily creating their own type of protective bubble. Then, slowly, in a soft voice, Ria prepared them to return from their cozy state. "When you are ready, gradually bring your attention to your body by moving it slightly. Breathe in alertness and smile."

Next, Ria invited the group to open their eyes when they were ready. Peeking out of one eye, elf saw smiles and heard giggles. It was like she and the sprites, elves, and fairy kids were glowing from inside. Even the sunlight brightened the sky as they came back from their meditation experience.

Everyone watched as Ria crawled upward on the branch, hung upside down, and spun a tiny silk thread to attach herself to the branch. Mesmerized, they observed her forming a "J" shape and wriggling to shed her outer caterpillar skin. A soft, sea-green shell formed over her innards. In awe, with a magical sense of wonder, they saw tiny gold dots appear in a ring around the shell.

Since Ria understood her purpose in living first as a caterpillar, she was ready for the changes that were happening to her. Curious, one of the braver sprites asked Ria if she was afraid of the changes that were taking place. Others chimed in too, having the same concern.

"I did feel threatened at first, but by focusing on my courage and the safe shelter that is holding me like a protective hug, I recognized I am really excited," answered a sleepy Ria. She yawned and wriggled once more, positioning her body for 10 days of stillness.

The elves and fairies yawned, too. They could sense a change coming for them as well. They wanted to trust that this mysterious experience was a visible expression of their own transformation. They were learning healing wisdom from their time spent meditating and then witnessing Ria's changes. They had learned that brain structure can change very rapidly when exposed to new stimulus, and that they were actually developing new pathways in their brains that opened them to expanding awareness for new perceptions and self-care. They savored the stillness they felt inside.

The deep peace stayed with them throughout the week as they integrated their broader awareness of questioning what could be possible. Fae introduced the idea of playing within one's bubble, which is an exercise from a meaningful, fun fitness dance called *Nia Technique®* or *Nia*. "You can create moves that stimulate the experience of joy in your body. The motion is healing, especially when you set the intention of imagining all your needs being met," offered Fae.

She reminded them that they could choose to keep the essence of their cocoon, chrysalis, egg shell, or bubble around them. "You can imagine this as your security "bubble" anytime you need it. Create this space and play in it by moving in circular motions inside your new protective shelter.

The group talked about all the options they could imagine as a safety bubble and how they could be used interchangeably. Some of them liked recreating a womb space to symbolize a fresh start. elf planned to use her cocoon for comfort when she would be lying down and a bubble when she'd be upright. The Safe Peeps all agreed that this week they had learned a lot about self-care and they wanted to meet back at the tree house in one week.

A Protective Practice

elf was elated to sense joy in her body, so she practiced forming the protective cocoon around her before she crawled out of her bed the next morning. As she lay in her tiny, fluffy bed, she moved her body parts in circular motions inside her bubble, as she repeated, "All my needs are fulfilled." She curled her knees toward her shoulders, then pulsed them away, and then in, again and again. This felt good, like a gentle, internal massage to her back and belly. She wrapped and unwrapped her arms as her legs twirled around each other. She repeated tightening her muscles—squeezing her bones and then letting go. It felt like a warm, nourishing, inner hug.

elf swirled her upper frame in the opposite direction of her lower body. This physical enveloping and unfolding moved her emotions as well. She transitioned through some fear and quickly into gratitude as she symbolically reclaimed her body as her own. This new sense of protection allowed her to enjoy moving more than she used to, because she now felt safer and more trusting of her body. Her energy was no longer stuck as it had been when her body held fear and depression in her cells.

elf was developing a new way of being, not only with her body, but with her emotions, thoughts, and spirit, too. Sliding like a silkworm out of her covers, she was aware of feeling more freedom than she had in years. She was determined to learn to feel safe everywhere she went. She affirmed, "All my needs are fulfilled!"

elf wrote in her journal about this creative movement and also about how she had felt when she had watched Ria transform her body. elf wondered if Ria missed her fuzzy striped caterpillar body or felt sad about leaving it behind. elf decided to ask Ria.

When elf found Ria, still encased in her protective sheath and hanging from the branch, she asked the questions that so puzzled her. Ria's answers did not come to elf in the usual way. It was as if Ria was talking inside elf's head, giving her subtle impressions. This different way of communicating absolutely intrigued and delighted elf. To get the inside messages from Ria, elf needed to be quiet and aware. A couple of deep breaths helped her access quiet awareness with ease.

Ria told elf that she had been sad and missed her caterpillar body, but that she had allowed the grief and sadness to move through her like a gentle breeze. Eventually, this act of letting go opened her to feel compassion for herself. She conveyed that she was honoring her spiritual journey and beginning to feel lighter.

elf appreciated that Ria taught her the importance of feeling emotions, and that when we do this, our feelings provide motion that propels us to the brighter feeling on the other side.

Ria's words arrived inside elf's head, "I almost feel like I am not really here—as if this transformation is magical. I believe that because I am surrendering to the process, a miracle is happening in natural time."

Overwhelmed and needing to relax, elf lay down on the soft, sun-warmed grass below the weeping willow tree. She remained curious about how Ria's changes were affecting her, and wanted to "hear" everything Ria had to say, but the safety of Mother Earth lulled her to sleep. She dozed into a lucid dream, feeling even freer than she had been in a long time.

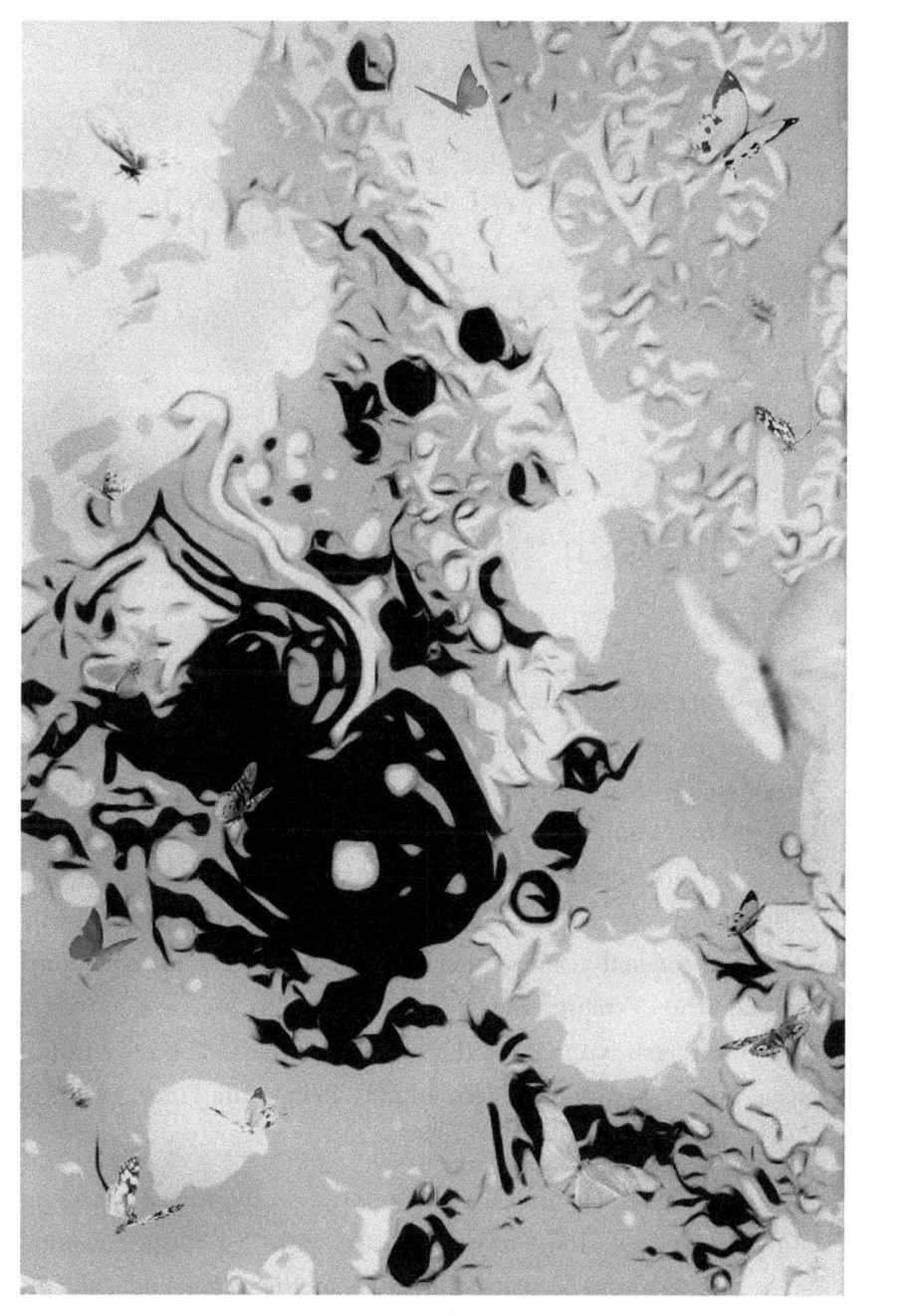

Chapter ~ 12 ~

Elf's Self Aligned with Source

Elf dreamt of a bursting pinky/peach sunrise that communicated with her in the inner way that Ria was able to communicate. In the dream, she was on the beach where her Godparents had taken her that summer. Prancing along, energized by the sun, she came upon some glistening shells deposited on the sand in the shape of a big "S." Intrigued, she ran her hand over the curvy texture of the shells. A message suddenly came to her through an inner voice. This inner voice said the "S" represented elf's connection to Source, the Creator of all—the forest, nature, and the entire Universe. Some refer to this Divine Source as God, Goddess, Infinite Being, Life Force, Spirit, or other names.

In her dream, elf used a stick to write words in the sparkling, diamond-like sand. The words all started with "S": Spirit, Sunshine, Safety, Strength, and Security. She wrote another big S, and suddenly the letters of her name, e...l...f, appeared after the "S". "Self," elf exclaimed in her dream, realizing her name was transformed and now held a greater and deeper meaning!

elf felt warm and tingly inside. Again and again she read the word Source had bestowed on her. Her heart reverently accepted its profound significance each time she uttered it. "Self... Self... Self!"

"S" was a powerful addition to her name "elf." As she began to perceive the deep-rooted meaning of the word, it helped her connect to that strong, Wise One within and in all things. She tuned into the gift of her wholeness as Self, and was confident that Self had greater perception than any individual part of her. She sensed that Self holds the potential energy to restore her various parts to wholeness.

In her dream state, elf could understand this complex impression. It honored her to know that she was a part of something much bigger, and that her life held real meaning and purpose. This newly revealed deeper Self was able to trust that all she needed to know would be revealed to her, at the right time. elf came to know, through this dream, that Self represents the capacity for wholeness in each individual and their connection as an Infinite Being.

In the vision, Source revealed this distinct message, "You have developed the awareness to remember who you really are. You become more whole each time you ask your Wise Self or tune in to you as an Infinite Being to assist any less mature or frightened part of yourself. The parts that were lost and repressed will, in time, naturally be re-membered—or reunited—as members into the real you."

Through this transformation in the way she related to herself, she recognized the importance of honoring who she is now by capitalizing the first letter of her name. The Self of Elf radiated with delight! She wanted to always remember her brilliant connection to this Source, this bigger Self, and all her dear parts. Elf's Self began to dance in spirals, celebrating with her inner Elf, promising to care for her always as a loving parent would do.

As Elf awoke, tears of joy welled up in her eyes. The center of her being radiated with hope. She saw that she was important, even if her parents never truly heard or saw her. Her Wise Self helped her remember that she mattered and inspired her to continue enlightening her parts through inner conversations with Self.

At that moment, she realized she had dozed off near Ria. She glanced up at the chrysalis that embraced Ria. Elf sensed that Ria had witnessed Elf's Self-awakening event, even if it was a lucid dream. Knowing someone witnessed it, magnified the importance of her transformation.

Little by little, as Elf awakened, she swirled her body inside her own cocoon again, imagining building a stronger Self. The light beamed into her fantasy as she imagined and sensed the cocoon cushioning her as she made circles with each of her joints. Her joints were seeking joy as she squeezed her muscles, embracing the pleasure of movement. Elf thoroughly reclaimed her body in this experience. She now realized and affirmed that her body was hers and only hers. "This is my body!" She hugged herself tightly as she rocked with elation over feeling empowered and very connected to her body.

When her body was ready to slink out of her made-up cocoon-like nest, she moved deliberately and stretched deliciously from her fingertips all the way through the cells of her reaching toes.

Then, she drew images of her vivid dream in her journal. She also practiced writing over and over, "Self" and "Elf" with capital letters. As she drew, she knew Elf and Self were connected with Spirit/Source. The more she drew, the stronger and happier she felt. Self fully accepted the imperfection that is involved in being an elf, and, at the same time, Self acknowledged her value by highlighting her name.

Self knew it would take some time to blend this new connection with Source into her daily life. "It's a good thing Self has patience," Elf scrawled in her journal.

Chapter ~ 13 ~

Detachment to Resolve the Pain

Elf was growing stronger and enjoying her life more. However, during one individual fairapy session, Elf was anxious and did not know why. Fae helped her realize it was just a part of her that was troubled and not the entirety of her being. That recognition helped her relax a smidgen.

This wise fairapist gently reminded Elf to breathe. Next, she asked Elf if her troubled part could step aside to give Elf some space. Elf took a few deep breaths as she inwardly posed the question to that part of her.

To Elf's surprise, that part agreed, leaving Elf feeling better. With Fae's support, Elf was then able to begin talking with her inner parts.

Fae thought this idea of connecting with inner parts might be confusing to Elf, so she took a moment to explain that the work they are doing is called *Internal Family Systems*. It really made sense to Elf when Fae further explained, "A younger part of you has been stuck back at the time of the abuse. That part does not know you are now older and safe! This is a normal and unfortunate effect of trauma—to have parts inside holding memories from a younger time, but, fortunately, this can be resolved with guidance."

Elf's Self updated the young part of her that was feeling scared. She shed tears of release and of relief when she understood that Self was there to care for her. Elf informed the newly aware part that she now had Safe Peeps, who hadn't been there when she was younger.

Elf took a couple of full breaths. In the silence, she sensed a deep change as she continued to create a new internal relationship that gave her young part safety. Contemplatively, she held a pillow to her chest and started to rock back and forth.

When Elf was ready to speak, Fae asked her to find out what the young part needed. Elf had an inner talk with her little elf and found out she needed more reassurance that she was safe and cared for, and that she wanted to be protected and nurtured because she was exhausted.

Elf shared that info with Fae, and Fae validated the importance of little elf's needs. They discussed how Elf could provide that support for her wee one and how often. Elf's Self could now show up to provide for her inner child, so the younger part no longer needed to take over with the feeling of panic.

Fae provided Elf with a leaflet that contained information on helping her inner child become whole after trauma. It defined trauma as a shocking event, injury, or ordeal. Elf was grateful to learn more about Self abilities and how to care for herself in this way.

Fae also shared a book with Elf to help her uncover more of her whole, joyful Self. Fae explained that the book by Schwartz (2001), *An Introduction to Internal Family Systems*, describes seven Self-qualities: curiosity, compassion, calmness, confidence, clarity, courage, and connection. Fae said there are additional ways to describe Self and assured Elf that they would play with those ideas in group sessions.

Elf wanted to practice the best Self-care for the well-being of all her parts. She now understood that because her younger parts had the courage and ability to keep the disturbing, prickly memories hidden from her awareness, they had helped her survive. She did not know how she would have been able to focus on her life, nor how she would have wanted to go on, had she been consciously aware every day of the overwhelming trauma. She was immensely grateful that her parts had saved her life. Now, her desire was to save them from the dark places they got stuck in, by helping them to talk about the memories inside.

Fae had encouraged the group to compile notes for a workbook to help them and other survivors to heal. This led to them eventually inviting me—the narrator and future guest storyteller—as a witness to support their writings. More from me later.

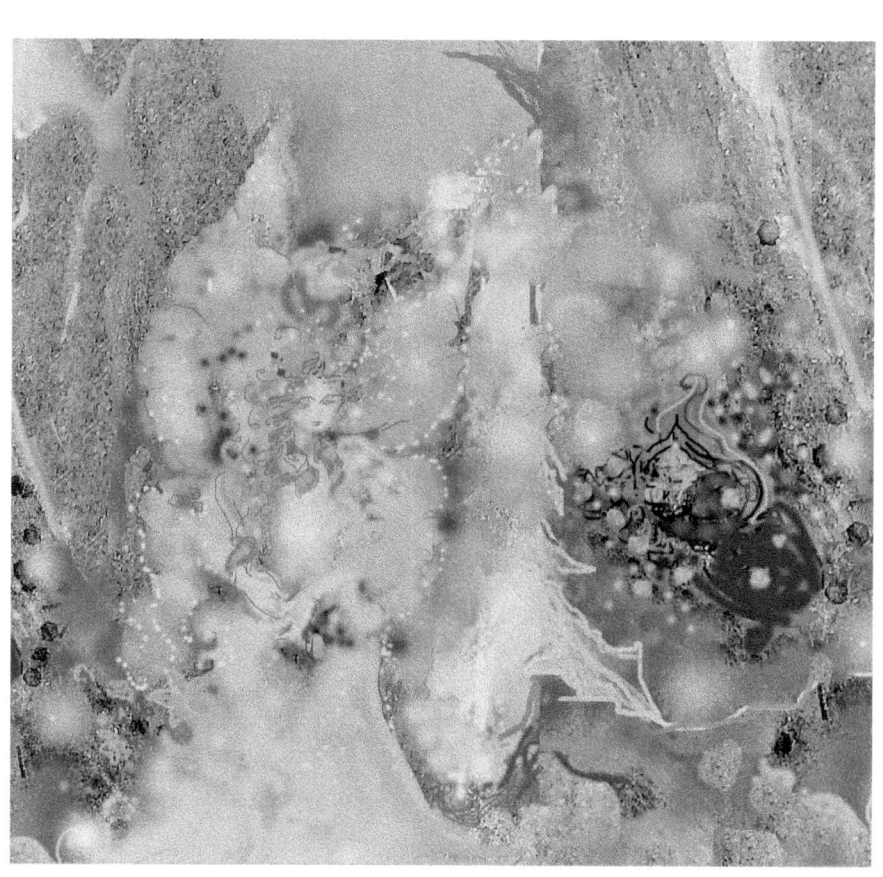

Chapter ~ 14 ~

Gifts of Self

The group met in a fairy ring to start learning about the gifts of the Wise Self. Fae explained, "Everyone has access to and can develop more awareness of these gifts." In these circles they read about Self characteristics, shared their stories, and at times even hosted a guest critter who came to visit and talk about the gifts of Self.

This time, Fae introduced a gray, long-haired cat named Carlyle. He had dark gray stripes all around his body and white fur covering his feet and ankles that made it appear as if he wore socks. Fae asked the group to warmly welcome him.

The group dynamic was different with a stranger present—they were guarded, even though his eyes looked sincere and quite magical. He seemed friendly, coming close to the teens as if waiting for them to pet him.

Fae introduced acceptance as the first topic, which included curiosity, a trait that can lead to many good things. "Acceptance opens your heart without judgment. Being curious hones your attention to the details of what you are accepting. And curiosity invites attention, interest, and inquisitiveness, which can grow into fascination."

Just then, Carlyle gracefully ambled into the center of the circle and silently took a cat stretch pose. He encouraged the group to experiment with long cat stretches as well. "Stretching your body models openness for your mind and prepares you for more flexibility in your thoughts and feelings."

Everyone enjoyed trying the cat stretch, so he lightheartedly engaged them in other stretches. He was here to help the group become curious about their inner parts and to tune in when they struggled. The playful exercises helped them get warmed up and readied them for the next step.

Fae shared that the group had been gaining awareness of parts of them. Carlyle nodded and asked them to become curious about their inner child parts. He continued to stretch—out of sheer enjoyment—encouraging them to do likewise.

Speaking very slowly, with a pause between each instruction, Carlyle said, "Use your imagination to pay attention to any subtle stirring inside that might be a message from your inner child. Slow down to be interested in really hearing and understanding what that hurt or deprived part may need. Listen inquisitively to the feelings of your hurt part. He or she was probably ignored when trying to tell others about being disrespected and hurt. Do not judge any emotions they share as wrong. Accept their feelings. Become fascinated with the part's ideas and views. And b r e a t h e."

Carlyle explained that youngins start their life innocent and well-intentioned, but fear and disappointment can cause them to get stuck, continuously reacting from past emotions. He shared an idea that would help them stretch past this jammed energy. "If you feel trapped by reliving confusion, pain, or fear, you can focus on becoming curiouser and curiouser! This is the first step to free you of past trauma. Experiment with it."

Most of the group closed their eyes as they searched their body to find some inner discomfort to become curious about. Elf noticed she could breathe deeper just by acknowledging some worry she had been holding inside and accepting it. It felt like a window had just opened inside of a stuffy closed-in room.

Then, Carlyle asked the "Peeps" to share ways they could create interest in their inner feelings, even when they felt unsettling emotions. Many said they noticed that as they gave this positive kind of attention to their inner child, the uncomfortable feelings softened.

As they talked, Carlyle sniffed and snooped around the circle, inserting his nose into their backpacks. Elf and the other young ones chatted and laughed about Carlyle's curiosity. He also nudged their hands the way cats do when they want to be touched. As they tenderly stroked his fur, Carlyle purred loudly. The soft, purring rhythm wooed the group like a lullaby. They felt linked to Carlyle and each other.

By observing Carlyle's energy, they got a sense of how to be curious and how to begin to accept what was going on inside of themselves. Fae asked the group what other positive inner traits could be created by this greater sense of acceptance.

The fairies and elves responded individually in their sing-songy voices: "Feeling safe inside." "Creating a new connection." "Learning something we didn't know about a part of us." "An unexpected surprise I call serendipity." "Feelings of love for my inner child." "A sense of belonging in the group." Elf added, "Acceptance brought calmness deep in my heart, and becoming fascinated with who I am inside led to feelings of fulfillment."

Carlyle gave the participants a lot of credit for their insights and for sharing the benefits of building internal acceptance. He also purred a heartfelt thank you for their acceptance and for trusting the mystery.

Fae brought closure to the session by acknowledging them for their willingness to be present, for being curious about their feelings, and for accepting their own feelings. "Accepting yourself is a healthy step toward restoring your wholeness."

UNWRAPPING MORE

The next week Elf and her circle of friends talked about Self gifts related to caring and compassion. Fae described compassion as deep caring, kindness, and consideration for someone or something. "Compassion develops with a mature or sacred intention, stirring pure goodwill in your heart center."

Just then, a rambunctious litter of pups ran roly-poly in to greet them! Elf giggled as she asked how the puppies could teach them caring and compassion. Fae suggested they stay curious and continue to observe.

An elf named Julio imitated a puppy that would nip and have mischievous bouts with another pup. The group laughed because they had witnessed how the pups' behavior was similar to Julio's behavior when he teased Anika, a feisty fairy in the group.

Julio admitted that when he began imitating the tiny whippersnapper, he recognized his own rowdy habit, and felt an inner TUG of compassion for the little guys. By observing them, he had more compassion for Anika. Surprised by a sudden insight, Julio exclaimed, "I just realized that I treat Anika badly when I am unhappy with myself, because Anika reminds me of what I feel inside. I react by picking on her instead of being inquisitive about my discomfort."

The group listened carefully. They realized that at times, they too, do something similar with their frustrations. Instead of accepting their hurt or anger, they acted out or felt irritated by someone else. Anika was surprised and relieved to hear that. She timidly shared that she would be so nervous when Julio pestered her that she would shake inside, but she was good at hiding her fear.

Meanwhile, the rollicking puppies calmed down, stretched out on their bellies, and played quietly. The subdued atmosphere was the perfect time for a soft-spoken fairy named Tender Heart to whisper that empathy—the ability to understand another's feelings or difficulties—was also vital. She shared that she believed empathy validated—confirmed the truthfulness and value of—her inner feelings.

Everyone in the group agreed they needed more empathy for their own feelings. Tender Heart said, "When my inner child's feelings are valued as a treasure, I'm able to generate love to, hmmm—to tend her heart."

Elf chimed in with a chuckle, "Get it? Tend-er Heart's message is to 'tend her heart'. I like that."

"Mmmmmmmm" was the sound Fae made to validate such an important insight. "Your name is a reminder to tend to the heart of your inner child."

The puppies had nestled together in a pile, but each time one would squirm, it would nudge the others, and they would all whine and wiggle until they could get comfy close to one another again. The puppy whimpers were unsettling to Anika. The Safe Peeps witnessed tough Anika suddenly becoming tearful. Risking being vulnerable, Anika shared, "I have a habit of protecting myself by acting outwardly harsh."

Fae asked what the vulnerable part of her would need to feel safe. Anika looked at her group of Safe Peeps. "I wish you could all comfort me the way the puppies nuzzle each other. I long for close contact that is safe," she explained in a soft, shy voice.

The fairy realm nestled close to Anika and in this supportive realm they made soothing, whimpering sounds like the puppies. Anika released contented whines as she was comforted by her considerate friends. The littlest pup crawled into the fairy circle and put his head on Anika's foot. She smiled and received the gift of his love.

While the group expressed care through the shared touch and soothing sounds, some of the Safe Peeps stayed to the outside of the cluster and only touched for a short time. They honored their own sense of comfort, trusting how much touch was right for them. Other friends wiggled and scooted, trying to determine their comfort level. Others felt safe cozily nesting within the group.

Anika said she could call on her tough part to protect her if she needed it, but for now she felt relief as her body melted into the fairies' version of the "puppy pile." She thanked everyone in the softest voice any of them had ever heard from her! She and Julio held hands and swayed. Fae commended Anika for having the courage to make a request for innocent comfort. "The sense of belonging is an important gift that boosts our ability to be our Self."

Julio questioned the meaning of Self, which he had done before. Fae asked him how he would like to refer to his connection to wisdom.

"Oh that! I call it TUG," Julio answered as if they knew who he was talking about.

"Tug???" the group questioned in unison.

"Yeah, the knowing ya have that tugs you in the direction that's best. The pull toward integrity and your purpose. TUG stands for The Ultimate Guide. That's who I listen to when I allow myself to surrender to my inner TUG. For reasons I don't understand, I often get in a 'Tug of War' with receiving the peace TUG has to offer. My life goes better when I open to the inner TUG."

The fairy ring was impressed and also curious about Julio's unique view. Fae honored his belief, showing she respected everyone's distinctive spirit. She said she would be glad to include The Ultimate Guide as one of the choices when referring to the Higher Wisdom. Julio beamed and gave a nod of his head.

Fae encouraged the Safe Peeps to continue nourishing their bodies, thoughts, feelings, and beliefs. "Fill any needy part with love and forgiveness whenever that part wants it. Warm it with gentleness and a blanket of safety."

Fae pointed to the puppy pile. "This is an example of what it is like when you are in a healthy and purposeful family. You rest in the feeling of belonging and kinship. Your group is like a loyal family that has bonded through understanding and honoring each other."

Some of the group members lived with relatives whose only bond was being in the same house. Sadly, this was because their parents and caregivers had rarely received concern when they were young ones themselves. They passed on the pain by ignoring their children when they were hurt, as they had been ignored.

What they were learning in group was helping Elf and her friends extend compassion to their families "if it was safe" and "only if" they were open to receiving it. Little by little, some families were becoming more considerate of each other. In others, distance provided a safe space.

Spring break had arrived, and with spring came a renewal of hope. The ground had softened, plants were sprouting, birds were cheerfully chirping, and nature was promising growth and change.

Chapter ~ 15 ~

Shell's Pain Needs an Outlet

Elf had been anticipating the special day when her aunt would take her to the ocean again. The day finally arrived. Elf was eager to find the little creature in the shell that she had befriended on her last visit to the ocean. Elf looked up and down the beach and finally found Shell. She had often thought about Shell and wrote about her in her journal.

"Shell, are you in there?" Elf gently asked. "I have some things to tell you." Elf was excited to share what she was learning in group, hoping it might also help Shell. Most of all, she wanted to show Shell how to practice more kindness toward herself.

"Yes," said a very small, hesitant voice.

To Elf, the voice sounded sad. With empathy, Elf asked, "Are you ok?"

"Nooo... Ouwie~Ouwie! Ouwieeeee!" came a sudden cry from Shell.

Elf was alarmed and asked Shell, "What is hurting?"

"My throat is very sore."

At first, it was tricky for Elf to follow Shell's train of thought, especially since Shell lowered her voice to a whisper.

"My throat started hurting because I was yelling. I so wanted the sea monster to hear me! I wanted him to know that I am a Being with feelings and he was hurting me! I wanted him to stop touching my privates!" The words tumbled out in a rolling sob. Elf kind-heartedly listened, recognizing Shell's deep layers of pain.

"My voice did not matter. That's what makes me feel sooo sad!!!!"

Shell's weeping slowly turned into a soothed murmur as Elf hummed a comforting, "Mmmmmm-Mmmmmmmmmm," and placed her hand on Shell to let her know she cared. Elf knew that abuse creates layers of heart-wrenching agony for the victim. These layers can be healed by finding and feeling the energy or emotion, and then releasing them.

Elf heard Shell taking deep calming breaths. Then, she heard a loud whoosh like a gushing wave each time Shell let the pain go. Stillness filled the air, and Shell shared that as she released the overwhelming sorrow, her anguish left with it. Elf acknowledged Shell's awareness of the emotions that were held inside her physical pain. "You tuned in so well to find important details. I am impressed with how wise you are, even when your emotions are throbbing!"

"Ree-eally?" Shell's voice cracked as she questioned in astonishment.

"Absolutely!" Elf confirmed! "You are learning so quickly, and I am very proud of you."

"Wow... Elf, I couldn't have done it without you. Your guidance is what gets me through the sticky muddle. I don't know how you get me to feel better, but I do feel better!"

"Thank you, Shell. You are doing more work for yourself than you realize. Letting yourself be aware of the emotions so you can release them is the most challenging part. There is always a light emotion on the other side of a heavy one." Saying these words helped Elf recognize what Fae meant when she said the same thing to Elf after some profound work.

Elf encouraged Shell to focus on what she wants to create and assured her she can wait until she feels ready. Elf explained, "Our attention does have power, so it is helpful to use our thoughts and emotions constructively after we have cleared the pain."

The only thing Shell wanted now was to rest in the sun. She was exhausted and ready for a nap. Shell took a long drink of water to help her dry throat.

"One other thing," said Shell. "You can call me Shelly. It suits the softened and open nature of who I really am. I feel brand new!" Then she closed her eyes and smiled blissfully. Her throat was already feeling better, relieved that her truth was acknowledged. Her heart felt delight over being heard.

Elf blew her a kiss as they said their goodbyes. "I am so, so proud of you, Shelly," added Elf.

"Ooooh, thank you!" Shelly exclaimed with immense gratitude. She was so grateful that Elf had really listened and understood her.

As Elf walked back to where her aunt was sitting in the sun, she was filled with gratitude for how honored she felt by her friend's trust in her. It had been uncomfortable for her parts to hear Shell's distress, but Self was able to soothe the part inside Elf that was feeling stress. Inside, Self promised to listen to that sensitive little elf part more.

When Elf got home, she wrote in her journal about the compassion she felt for her tender little elf part. Her elf part felt validated. Her young part, who was reminded of her own past pain while talking to

Shelly, now wanted to be hugged. Elf began to understand that her Self is able to respond from a whole space when she can tune into infinite resources of Source energy. She was grateful that she was connected to her strong Self to now provide love for her younger part. With all her heart, she wrapped her arms around a pillow and rocked her little elf. She thanked her inner part for being so incredibly patient while Elf gave her attention to Shelly.

The next couple of times Elf and Shelly got together, they had great fun playing in the shallow water. Life felt oh so good! Shelly shared that she replayed their prior healing conversation many times in her mind. This new experience helped her feel safe enough to come out of her shell for short periods and make more friends.

Elf had thought Shelly was physically connected to the shell she lived in. She was excited about adventures they could experience now that Shelly was moving about! Elf was also surprised to see that Shelly was a lovely and shapely water sprite. Bewildered, she asked Shelly why she hid in the shell.

Shelly got quiet and self-conscious, "I am uncomfortable about my body being noticed. I thought I would be in danger without the shell. It makes me feel safe," explained Shelly.

Elf understood what she meant and knew how important it is to feel safe. She shared that she, herself, shuts down and goes into a "shell" inside. Recognizing another bond they shared, they just smiled and looked into each other's welcoming soul eyes.

While looking into Shelly's eyes, Elf was surprised to notice something deeper, as if Shelly was hiding some pain. Elf did not have words to ask or understand what she sensed. Clearly uncomfortable to be more vulnerable, Shelly distracted them with some babble about the weather and then it was time to say goodbye. Elf was concerned and hoped Shelly wasn't hiding something detrimental.

Unlimited Heart

Elf was experiencing her own ups and downs. Yet, the down times did not seem as low as they used to be, and feeling fully alive happened most of the time. Elf focused on the good times, often reminiscing about how joyfully her friend Susie Q lived her life. Susie Q was especially clever at identifying the strengths she gained from life's challenges. Her radiant spirit was contagious and taught Elf a lot about the rewards of a positive, authentic attitude.

Elf learned to accept the rough times as an opportunity to care for herself. She would practice listening to her inner thoughts and feelings. Then she would acknowledge and attend to what she needed. She found that increasing her patience for her feelings—and understanding how trauma had fragmented her self into several parts—had no limits. When she tended to her feelings from her heart, her love and patience grew and grew. She cherished knowing her mature and Wise Self when she did this.

Elf had learned from a healer that the deep heart develops if one chooses to progressively mature. To Elf, that meant she had the full potential to heal anything that hurt inside of her. The whole process took more time than she expected, yet she was also learning to gently and patiently trust natural time.

The healer was known as Mother Sage. She was a garden angel with a bit of a wild spark, a *Reiki* energy healer, a knowledgeable advisor, though too mysterious to understand on a rational level. When Elf asked questions, Mother Sage frequently asked Elf what she knew.

Elf liked sharing her awareness, and enjoyed the confidence boost when the healer responded to Elf with something like, "Exactly! I like your creativity," or she'd give a cryptic answer that prompted deeper soul research.

Experiencing Mother Sage left Elf wanting to know more from her, especially about the deep heart. Mother Sage shared her opinion, "Most people make decisions from their surface heart, which is immature and reaches outwardly to fill many random wants. They don't know how to discover and prioritize what would benefit their true purpose for being on earth."

Mother Sage pointed to the center of her own chest and continued, "The deep heart is located behind one's sternum in the center of the chest. Pressing your hand there as you meditate will help you sense your potential and your heart's infinite gifts, including your authentic purpose. It takes time to cultivate the ability to access one's deep heart."

This left Elf curious about the mystery in her heart center. She felt hopeful that she had a meaningful purpose to fulfill. She sensed a stirring in her heart center when she followed Mother Sage's suggestion to meditate with one or both hands there.

At first, Elf felt tightness. Then, she sensed some grief in the area of her sternum. As she breathed, the tightness softened, tears rolled out, and the sadness melted. The gentle, rousing movement within transformed itself into warm loving energy.

This meditation became a ritual she practiced as she dozed off to sleep each night. It created secure Self energy for the next day.

Replacing Judgment with Curiosity

Some time passed before Elf got to see Shelly again. When she did, Elf was disappointed that Shelly felt miserable. A part of Elf judged Shelly for not taking better care of herself. She even talked to Shelly in a tone that scolded her. It offended Elf when Shelly responded in an angry tone. To Elf, this sounded like the immature version of "Shell". Elf wanted to leave.

Then suddenly, Elf remembered how much she had hurt when someone ignored a part of her that got stuck in pain. Elf realized she was making the situation worse by judging Shelly. Elf apologized and explained that before she could really listen in the ways Shelly needed, she would have to care for her own parts. "Perhaps if I go for a walk, I will feel better myself and be able to care about you when I return."

Shelly started to cry tears of joy. "You would do that for me?"

"Of course!" was Elf's reply.

As Elf walked on the beach, she became aware that she had been holding her breath. She had not expected Shelly to be so sad again. A part of Elf worried that healing does not last. To let go of that fear, Elf focused on courage as she connected with her stronger Self. The sun's skin-tingling warmth reassured her of her connection to Source.

Elf's Wise Self recognized that Shelly might be experiencing feelings she'd had to hide in the past. Her Wise Self was curious and wanted to ask Shelly questions to better understand her feelings. Elf was ready to allow her Wise Self to lead the conversation with Shelly.

Elf returned to Shelly and spoke warmly with the troubled Shell, hoping she was giving Shell an opportunity to open up. Elf calmly waited, then intently listened when Shelly blurted out what was distressing her so.

Wanting to Die

Shelly cried, "The sea monster that I told you was hurting me..." Through tears she continued, "He is my foster dad. He is the one who has been touching private areas of my body at night. I was confused about who it was, partly because I didn't want to believe it myself, but now I kno-o-o-ow.

"The problem got worse when I tried to tell my foster mom what happened. She didn't want to hear it. She told me to stop making up crazy stories. I began to doubt myself. I thought she must be right! Something must be wrong with me for making up stories that she called crazy!"

Elf shared that she felt the same way until Fae and others explained that young ones don't make up these stories of sexual abuse. "If that is how you remember the events, that is your truth and you need to believe what you know. It sounds like your foster mom is in denial and not able to hear your truth. I am so sorry for that," Elf said, and gave Shelly a big hug.

Elf knew what it was like. "There is a lot of loneliness when your family ignores you that way. I believe you—and responsible, caring people will, too! You need to find a safe adult who can help you and make sure the abuse comes to an end. Can you do that?"

"I don't know," sobbed Shelly. "I don't want to live anymore. It's too painful!"

Elf held the shell and rocked her until she settled. "I know it is so painful. I also know that it is just a part of you that does not want to be here. At times I have seen you really enjoy living. Besides, I want you to live! A healer I met along the way helped me understand that the wish to end your life is really the desire for something in your life to end. Of course, you want the abuse to stop! You need your brave Self to stand up for you and find a safe adult who can support you and put an end to the abuse. You need some more Safe Peeps. You are worth it! The violation of your body needs to stop!"

Shelly stopped crying. She became calm and thanked Elf for helping her clarify her feelings. Shelly's Confident Self acknowledged, "I really do want to live. And I really want the invasion of my body to stop."

They both paused, listened to the ocean waves, and took some deep breaths. "Okay, Elf. I will get some help, right away. Thank you! I needed you to believe me. That is giving me the courage to take that step."

Elf was relieved that Shelly was going to get help. They said their goodbyes. Elf patted the shell, saying, "You are always in my heart, Shelly."

Elf returned home still concerned about Shelly. She imagined light around Shelly in hopes that she'd be safe, and contacted Fae to report the abuse. Fae said she had connections in that area and promised to follow-up, which was a big relief for Elf.

At her next session, Elf talked with Fae about how she responded to Shelly's ordeal. Elf had not recognized how well she handled the situation until Fae commended her for being a compassionate resource for her friend in dire need of help.

"Elf, you showed up fully present from your Wise Self, and sharing your story gave Shelly a wonderful example to follow. You are accessing wisdom from your Infinite Being. You have awareness and understanding that many survivors could benefit from."

Fae continued to express gratitude for Elf's willingness to assist others. "Now, take time to balance the care you provided by doing something light, like dancing for the joy of it! Celebrate what you've accomplished and trust that good outcomes are on their way."

The next evening, Elf gathered with Mother Sage and some friends to dance in a circle around a bonfire. Drummers provided rhythm while crickets and frogs played the melody. Fire fairies guided Elf to make use of the transforming magic of the fire and the earth. Their dancing feet and strong emotions drummed the thudding beat into the earth.

With every step, each sole of Elf's bare feet rhythmically connected with the cool ground. She felt the energy of the soil absorbing any remaining worry. Her soul energy—moving through her soles—penetrated deeply meeting the earth's soul energy in communion. Delight vibrated through her soles up into her bones, her heart, and her unique soul. This celebration freed Elf's spirit and contributed to her co-hearts as well.

Chapter ~ 16 ~

Emerging Butterfly!

For Ria, her transformation inside the chrysalis as a pupa was complete. As if coming out of a deep meditation, she became aware of her "being" stirring. She could barely budge inside the tight casing. Her body began to gently rock. Her urge to stretch and expand grew, but the tight shell hugging her constricted her movement.

Ria rested when she got tired. Then the deep need to unfold pushed through her body again and Ria nuzzled her head against what had been her sleeping bag. As her body lengthened, it tore the protective cocoon open at the bottom, exposing her to the cool air. She sensed that her body was completely different than before. The core of her swollen body pulsed, gradually pumping life-giving fluid into the veins intricately woven throughout her wrinkled wings.

She felt a rush of excitement; whatever had developed felt totally authentic. Gripping the torn edges of the shell with her new legs, Ria embraced a moment of complete stillness. She needed to regain her strength after exerting such intense effort to come into the light. She realized that her true Self was advancing to create an adventurous life.

Curious about Ria, Elf and some of her friends had encircled the pupa hanging from the weeping willow branch. Mesmerized, they had watched as it split open and a bug-like creature emerged. They stood in disbelief, not recognizing the colorful, crumpled form. They were in awe as bright orange wings unfolded.

Elf studied the beautiful insect closely. She noticed the thousands of tiny, delicate, overlapping scales that appeared to be painted orange with white spots on the wings, and the black veins that formed a strong framework. The tiny hairs on the inner body reminded Elf of how Ria's whole body had been covered with furry hair when she was a caterpillar.

When Ria moved again, she twitched her swollen body and wobbled. Fae appeared as if by magic, softly encouraging Ria, "You're doing well. Just trust your body." The worried group was relieved to hear Fae say that. Now they remembered that Ria could follow her body's inclinations. Ria slowly opened and closed her wings.

The rest of the Safe Peeps arrived and the group expanded their circle so all could observe this miracle of transformation. Ria welcomed their interaction, though her focus was on strengthening her wings. A few asked why Ria was unsteady and if she now knew how to fly.

Fae asked the group to discuss the extraordinary process that Ria had experienced. They enthusiastically chatted about how she had been a fuzzy worm that transformed inside a shell that until recently held her tight. They reflected on how her changes were unseen and had occurred slowly over time.

Ria shared how vulnerable she'd felt as a pupa, unable to protect herself, and how weak she felt after her struggle to emerge from the chrysalis. Ria explained, "The small hairs on my body are still sensory, only now I have longer legs that are sensitive to feeling as well. I have longer antennae with tiny knobs on the end that are also feelers. I can wave them around to sense my surroundings. I am excited that my wings will free me to fly wherever I want to go. But first, I need to adjust to this new way of being in the world."

The Peeps stepped in closer, still pondering the butterfly's journey from being a caterpillar, becoming a pupa, and being transformed during the chrysalis stage. Ria acknowledged that their loving attention helped her to be stronger. She tested her wings by fluttering to a flower petal. She rested until she regained strength. The caring group cheerfully whispered encouraging words.

When she was ready, Ria lifted off as if floating on the wind. She disappeared into the sky and then swooped down, fluttering around the circle. She gracefully landed on each friend in a gesture of gratitude. She spoke confidently, "By witnessing my new life, you have helped me value myself as I adjust to this new expression of who I am."

The fairies in the group took flight with Ria, playing on waves in the wind. The rest of the fairy realm could see Ria in the distance landing on a bright orange poppy. As she settled, it looked like Ria had disappeared. Her wings lay spread, camouflaged on the blossom. Very slowly, her wings lifted and then gently joined the flower again.

The group marveled over their sense of oneness with the wistful sight. They remarked how their encouragement had contributed to Ria's confidence as she struggled through rebirthing herself. Fae suggested they journal about how Ria's passage may relate to their own process.

Elf exuberantly exclaimed that she wanted to act out Ria's journey and admitted she felt envious of Ria's ability to fly. The group mused that, for elves, pretending to fly might be the next best thing. So they started out by exploring how it felt to shimmy on the ground like caterpillars. Then they scrunched up to imitate a chrysalis and rested.

They imagined themselves emerging transformed, spreading quivering wings, and finally testing them out for flight. They danced on tiptoes and ran with arms stretched, opening their hearts as they lifted their chins. The fairies fluttered and hovered over the elves as they pretended to fly.

Fae asked them about the importance of being still at times. With that thought-provoking question, she encouraged them to be still and journal their thoughts and feelings about what they experienced. Fae asked them to explore how their own transformation feels as they work through feeling bound by the after-effects of abuse, striving to be free themselves.

They daydreamed and doodled examples of how they have become freer and how they hoped it would become natural to experience more joy. Fae asked them to create a feeling of gratitude for all the freedom they hope for, as if it had already happened. Fae explained, "Scientific research has shown that gratitude is the key emotion to bring your future desires closer."

In the next gathering, Julio shared that he was perplexed about Ria's new adventure. "Is it only for fun? Are there any other purposes to a butterfly's life?" he inquired. Fae suggested he ask Ria. They looked for her and found her flitting on the tops of wildflowers.

Ria respected Julio's question and responded by showing how her coiled, sucking mouthparts enabled her to feed on nectar from a flower. She explained, "In the process of moving from one flower to another, I transfer pollen from one blossom to another. Many plants depend on butterflies like me as well as bees and moths for pollination. While I nourish myself, the pollen grains (the male sperm) stick to me and are transferred to the stigma (the female part) of the same or another ready and welcoming flower. After I transfer the pollen, fertilization of new life takes place, forming seeds that can then be released into the air. If the seeds land in a good spot, reproduction takes place and new plants will grow!"

Fae asked the group if they could understand how sexual pollination is a natural, innocent act. And of course they could. This had given them great appreciation for all that Ria and other insects do to spread the beauty of flowers. Fae shared, "I feel joy knowing that plants share nectar, and insects and birds do their part to spread even more beauty in the world to delight us. That is an example of how we are all part of the whole. When we notice, appreciate, and interact with nature, do you sense that we add to the magnificence?" The group nodded and smiled.

They inhaled the fragrance of the wildflowers. Some chose to pick a few to take home. Others believed it was important to leave the flowers connected to the earth. All choices were made with the intent of respecting the whole miracle of life. Everyone's vibration was lifted as they recognized their sense of belonging with their Earth family in all of nature! The group left with a remembrance of their own innocence, recognizing how sensual beauty deserves to be honored.

Chapter ~17~

New Beginning

It was a pleasure to be invited as the next guest mentor at Fae's group. As the narrator of this story, you would not guess who I am. I am the keeper of stories, and I represent powerful expression. Fae introduced me to the Safe Peeps as having a trait in common with them, since they are also powerful keepers of stories.

I tenderly made eye contact with each one in the group before I started, "I am sad that the teens in this group had to keep secrets as youngsters. You were not allowed to talk about what had happened to you." I paused, wanting to make sure they felt safe with me. "I care for the stories of others as a mystic—wizard-like—healer and storyteller. Considering the kind of animal I am, it's surprising that I feel this exceptional bond with storytelling, since I am not typically considered a social creature."

In my usual deep voice, I explained, "I am Badger, caretaker of much light and knowledge. I teach the skills of self-acceptance—being comfortable with one's self—and self-reliance—trusting yourself.

Beings can call on my badger energy to gain wisdom from their stories and to develop self-expressiveness and assertiveness. I hope to inspire you to tell your story by creating a fresh, new beginning.

"When Fae consulted me about speaking with all of you bright fairies and elves, we recognized some of you have been through harder times as young children than some individuals ever experience. I'd like us to get to know each other in a playful activity to provide a safe container, so you will be free to express any parts of your story that need empathy, witnessing, or deep caring."

The group spiritedly began a game of Follow the Leader, meandering and giggling as they joyfully moved toward an open area and frolicked over the grassy fields. Everyone got a turn to lead. The elves had learned from Ria that spinning and rolling one's body creates transformation, so when they had climbed a hill, the elves and the fairies lay prone and rolled down the grassy hills.

Elf led them by example to lay still at the bottom to experience the supportive grounding of the earth beneath them. They could feel Mother Earth absorbing old hurt feelings. The fairies were amazed to mystically experience the hurt being drawn out of them and asked me how that could happen.

I explained, "Mother Earth soaks up old hurt feelings and recycles them for a better use, since she is naturally a great recycler! Mother Earth will also compassionately cradle your bodies." I encouraged them to practice "Earthing" after I explained, "Earthing, or grounding, is the practice of connecting with Earth's natural electrical field. Doing this will detoxify your body, mind, and emotions. It may help to think of it this way—when you take apart the word 'Earthing,' you get 'Ear-thing.' I often practice actively listening to the earth by placing my ear near the ground. She whispers deep intentions of calmness and draws those listening to let go of their stress."

I noticed that a male fairy in Fae's group kept some distance away from the others and resisted staying on the earth. I was concerned. He didn't seem to get as much joy as the female characters who reawakened their senses through their connection with the earth and danced after grounding. I saw him fold his arms as he watched the wingless elves respond to the light energy that flowed from the winged fairies. He shook his head as they tip-toed and flitted over the ground. He sighed when they held the fairies' hands, which lifted their bodies and their spirits.

I confided in Fae, "Seeing this makes me wonder how I can help boys share their stories with other male survivors. Males handle situations differently than females. They need other male support to shift their narratives and become fully alive to themselves. Now I know what my next book needs to address."

Elf was amazed by the joy of feeling buoyant and weightless compared to the heaviness that still weighed her down for spells. The fairies glowed like bright, purple lights, which left the elves sparkling. The lightness gave Elf a glimpse of the possibilities ahead. She wanted the memory of this experience to stay with her. It resonated with her inner spark and graced her with a higher perspective.

They all giggled as they floated back to earth, because the grass wiggling in the wind tickled them. Joy filled the air and radiated to every creature around. They were learning to have fun while they moved through the stages of healing.

Using my badger senses to mentor Fae's group, I tuned into the burdensome negative energy carried by these abused members of the fairy realm. I recognized the flightiness of some of the members who had learned to distract themselves from feeling emotions. For those members of the group, this pattern had started when they were abused because it had been overwhelming to feel emotions. Now, the pattern was a habit, even though they no longer needed that protection in safe places. They were just beginning the process of gaining awareness as they experienced safety, acceptance of their emotions, healthier boundaries, and a greater range of feelings.

Through play, we were teaching a new model for functioning in a grounded way. They were learning to lighten up and detach from a past that tended to drag them down. The experience was productive and helpful for the participants, yet it disturbed me that such an ordeal had ever taken place in their lives.

When group time came to a close, I just wanted to retreat back into the earth. Although badgers do not hibernate, when something intensely traumatic in a culture needs digesting, we need to go deep to listen closely to the earth. We were near my burrow, so I pointed out the pile of dirt next to my entry. I let Fae know I would return next season, but first I needed to conjure up what I could do to prevent sexual abuse.

On my way home, I stomped into the earth to let out the tension I felt. I was angry that sexual abuse continued to harm innocent souls. As I descended into my sacred underground burrow, I sank into the sadness of recognizing such pain. I knew of the pain, as I have long collected the stories. Only, today, through the close connection with the survivors, I sensed just how excruciating it had been for them. As I snuggled into the comfortable dirt bed in my hideaway, tearfully I thought about the courage it took for the fairy realm to trust me with their wounded hearts. The deep desire in my tears was to stop future abuse. Asking the earth, as if in prayer, I questioned whether ending abuse was possible.

Answers came over time in dreams as I listened deeply to responses from the earth. The dreams showed me ways I could begin to build a network of badgers and other animals to stop the abuse by chasing perpetrators/abusers to a distant land. Badgers do not normally get along with other animals, even other badgers, so reaching out to ask for cooperation was a stretch beyond my comfort limit. It was a goal that would take much dedication, because it meant learning to communicate better socially in give-and-take ways I never thought possible.

The message I sensed as I listened to the wisdom of the earth, is that eventually systems could be put into place to educate the abusers about justice, accountability, boundaries, and respect. I recognized that my job as a storyteller meant getting the message to other animals to help them understand the importance of joining together to activate boundaries to protect youngins. I also learned that there already were many others learning and working to create a safer environment for our youth, the entire fairy realm, and beyond.

I now understood that fairies tend to be earth angels who assist all of life when they feel healthy, safe, and present. They help the plants, trees, air, weather, water, stones, fire/spirit, and animal kingdoms to evolve. They are ahead of human beings in their ability to cooperate. They help humans advance in their consciousness of their own and others' needs, thereby restoring wholeness among all the members of society. They use what they learn to provide lessons for others to follow if they are open to learning. It takes grounding and lightening up to receive guidance from these earth angels for putting a prevention plan into place. I will return to this topic later.

Chapter ~ 18 ~

Elf's Plight and Purpose

Elf relished how freely she played after learning and sharing with her friends in Fae's group. Her expanding freedom inspired her to reach out to help others. Her growing confidence showed—her body stood taller; her face radiated her sense of security. Being seen and acknowledged by me, a badger with such a physically strong, yet emotionally insightful presence, was like a mirror reflecting her soul essence and purpose. She recognized only the energy of this; the mystery of it was perplexing and even more intriguing!

Using her heightened sense of curiosity, she wondered what I knew about her. Longing to embody her soul essence by bringing her purpose through her soles—her steps in life—she sought me out. She wanted to ask me what I noticed about her, hoping it would help her feel even more secure if she understood herself better.

Despite feeling stronger, a part of Elf was leery of trusting me because of a rumor she had once heard. Someone had told her that I scared a couple of elves who were just toddlers, by showing my fangs and hissing. Unfortunately, she heard only part of the story. I was actually protecting them, and they misunderstood my actions. Days later, when Elf had time to meander, her heart prompted her feet to walk to my burrow. You see, although parts of Elf were timid, her Self had courage to take action.

I raised my head from my den as she timidly approached. "Oh," she said, sounding surprised to see me. "Hhhuh...hello," she stammered. "I was wondering if you might be willing to talk with me? I sensed you saw a deeper part of me, and I've wondered what you might know about my story. For some reason, I felt so different when I was near you."

"Really?" I asked, admiring her truthfulness. "In what way did you feel different?"

"Well," Elf responded in her melodic voice, "I felt like I was really seen by you, which made me feel confident. I was also captivated by your genuine interest in our stories. Yet..." She hesitated and then whispered, "I also feel kinda scared of you. I'd never seen a badger before the day you came to our group."

Empathically I replied, "I know I sometimes have a forceful demeanor, but my intention is to help you and the group feel secure with me."

I gave her time to calm herself, and then explained, "I detect that you might be afraid of me because you heard a rumor about me frightening a couple youngins. First, I want you to know that years ago, when you put your heart into telling your parents what Ug had done to you, you sent a message out to the Universe. I was the one who heard it. I regret that I heard about it after harm was done to you, but it did alert me to Ug's pattern of trapping youngins underground for abuse. I tuned in to his movements and attacked him when I found him sneaking up on a couple of very young elves. I am sorry that my fury toward Ug scared the elves. They were too young to understand that I prevented Ug from molesting them."

Elf was shaking her head, aghast at how the rumor had twisted the truth. I reassured her, "Elf, when you were a little tyke and told your mother and grandmother, the strong emotional plea for someone to protect you reached me. I didn't want any other youngins to be abused by Ug. Your courage to speak up made a difference. I want you to know I am sorry that your parents did not support you. I know that felt like a terrible rejection and caused you to often second-guess yourself."

Elf's eyes were wide, blinking continuously in amazement. Her mouth opened—without words to follow. Hitherto, she did nod her head.

After giving her time to absorb what I had said, I continued. "I chased him to the coast with the help of a skunk who marked him with his acrid stench and threatened him with more if he ever tried to come back. Skunks are so good at insisting on respect. His whole skunk family is still on the lookout for Ug, but I think Ug is too terrified to return. He escaped by boat to an island for sex offenders. It is a place where children, for their safety, are not allowed to go."

Elf was quiet for a long time. She became very sleepy. This was so much information to process. I could tell she was moving into a state of trust, gratitude, and admiration as her fear melted. With tears welling in her eyes, Elf acknowledged that I had risked my reputation when the young elves misunderstood my fierce anger. "Stopping Ug was the right thing to do!" She exclaimed quickly.

I could sense that Elf felt a meaningful bond with me. I was kin to her. She could barely get out the words, "Th...th...thank you." Her eyelids drooped and her body seemed to fold as she whispered, "I need to find a place to nap."

Emphasizing my purpose, I shared, "It is an honor to assist the innocent who are in trouble or harmed, and I want to support making a change in order to provide a safe future for all children."

In a determined voice I said, "You did not deserve the abuse you endured. It happened to you because you were at a vulnerable age, without protection. He took advantage of you because of his insane need to wield power over someone. He was a coward, addicted to disordered urges. His actions were wrong. The wrong behavior had nothing to do with anything you did."

Despite her fatigue, Elf was grateful that I addressed her shame before she left. I concluded by helping her imagine the future. "You can constructively use your anger by directing it toward severing—cutting and separating—yourself from the experiences that felt like punishments. You carried the shame. Perhaps by viewing the abuse you suffered as unfortunate accidents for you, you may be able to remove your subconscious perception that the blame was yours. It was never your fault. The shame was never yours, though I see how you got that message."

I breathed a heavy sigh, "Hhhhahhh," and continued, enunciating each word firmly. "Finding the fitting interpretation for yourself sets you free from blaming yourself. Yet, know there may be layers of shame to work though, as unfortunately, it was planted so deeply.

"Your belief that it was your fault needs to be fully uprooted. The offender is at fault; it was not an accident for him. It was a choice. The Universe conspires to repair the damages done by the offender and to nudge communities to shine the light of truth. If the offender chooses to face the harm he has done, his soul will have the opportunity to grow. That is a bigger conundrum than you need to deal with."

Elf breathed deeply, thinking about others who could learn from all the healing work she had done. Her heart longed to help others heal, yet she often judged herself as insignificant and unworthy to assist in such an important job. Hearing that her cry had a positive, unexpected effect, deeply impacted her. She started changing the way she saw herself. She asked the Universe to support recovery of her wholeness and the wholeness of others. She asked me if there was anything she could do to help other survivors.

I answered with a soul-purifying question. "What will move you forward in your life?" I waited until I saw the spark in her spirit that told me Elf got the essence of my question. "That's it! It's that energy that will lead you."

I encouraged her, "Create an intention that provides for your needs and your gist for joy. When you keep your well-being and your truest nature in the lead, believing that you deserve a good life, you also inspire others to bring their heart through their soles—as in—their feet! They generate love through their body, and connect it to their life on earth. They aspire to create a life they love to step into, by their soul choices!"

The serene look on her face told me that my words and wisdom opened Elf to see her unique gifts, so I concluded, "And Elf, acknowledge you, where you are already being you and inspiring others."

Chapter ~ 19 ~

Centering—Calm Focusing

Elf pined to experience more joy, and became aware that every time she shut down it stole her joy. She reflected on her need to express herself instead of freezing. In the stillness, a ray of light revealed a gift—her gift of finding and sharing insights when they were welcome.

Elf often helped other Safe Peeps discover nuggets of inspiration silenced underneath the load of shame that goes with abuse. She tended to take her in-depth understandings for granted, so it helped that Fae and the other survivors affirmed that her insights are a gift. They acknowledged her desire to help others, not wanting them to suffer silently as she had. This inspired Elf to focus on tuning in to Spirit for help when she knew that asking spot-on questions would lead others to grow in awareness of themselves.

Elf also cherished the potential of storytelling to help survivors of childhood sexual abuse heal. As she imagined producing a resource for readers that could transform their own personal story, tears of joy mushroomed in her eyes and a warm sensation expanded in her heart center. She envisioned creating an interactive journaling workbook for victims to help them become strong, fully alive survivors.

She wondered if Fae's group would be willing to get involved in developing a book that could help survivors empower themselves. She hoped to include Fae's leaflets, since Fae had suggested finding multiple uses for them.

Exhilarated by the dream of writing this book, Elf jotted down ideas to share with her Safe Peeps. Her plan was to first share what she aspired to create and then ask if they would share what helped them as they worked to reclaim their wholeness.

Elf was a natural teacher; hence, her enthusiasm grew as she prepared to teach others what she was learning. She acknowledged that her desire to share could certainly be considered a gift—a gift to herself and to others.

Elf wrote in her notes:

> I aspire to grow in awareness of my Self gifts and use them more in my day-to-day life situations. I know that repetition is important to form a new habit, so I will make it an ongoing growth practice to accept and love myself. My desire is to make the Journal Workbook interesting and fun for myself and for readers!

Elf found a comfortable place to sit near some blueberry bushes. She picked some teensy, weensy wild blueberries, which she kept in the cap of an acorn to nibble on while she started this fantasy project. Lying on a blanket in the cool, green grass, she closed her eyes and took mindful breaths. When she was ready, she etched these thoughts on some large, shiny leaves.

CENTERING

Centering is relaxed focused attention on being peaceful. To get centered, you may need to grow quiet inside with an activity like yoga, walking, or music. This aligns you with your inner spark—as in a glowing, pilot light that always stays lit—for a sense of balance. If there is chaos around or inside of you, you may need to make adjustments to obtain greater balance. Being centered is like the "calm in the eye of a storm." Try this exercise when you feel troubled and desire peace. (Start with a minor issue until you build skill with this technique.)

- ❖ Take a few deep breaths. Bring in calmness as you inhale. Release any tension as you exhale.
- ❖ Sense your body relaxing.
- ❖ Invite a younger part of you to rest in the safe space you create.
- ❖ Become curious and take time to get to know that part or your inner feelings.
- ❖ How does that part (or your feelings) want to be comforted?
- ❖ How can you support that need for comfort?

Elf tested the exercise for the Journal Workbook on herself. After she settled in and centered, Elf's Self asked what ways her part wanted to be comforted. In the quietness, she sensed a need for little elf to be held. Tenderly, Elf—Self—folded her arms in an embrace as if she were holding her young inner elf and soothing her. This part, too young to talk, conveyed with an impression that she needed to be rocked to the sound of humming.

Elf took some slow, deep breaths into her belly. She gently stroked her hair. She could sense her younger elf part feeling comforted. She promised little elf that she would cuddle her and rock her like this, or imagine the activity of rocking her inside, whenever she needed it. It might even help to cuddle with a stuffed animal. Then she thanked her younger elf part for letting her know what she needed.

Elf wrote this example in her own journal so she'd remember to check in with her young part. She practiced this Journal Workbook exercise almost daily until relaxing became natural. Her relaxation brought more awareness of her feelings.

Although she enjoyed writing the Journal Workbook, this work required spending a lot of time alone. She was lonely and struggling with a lack of confidence, so she followed up on a suggestion from Fae to reach out to friends when she was turning inward. She missed Susie Q and her friends from group. She realized that time with them reinforced her confidence. Perhaps she'd share her project with them. It might even help them build their own self-esteem.

As the Safe Peeps gathered, they played with friendly chipmunks who gave them speedy rides along paths through the woods. Sounds of glee and giggles abounded, along with the high pitch chirps of the critters. Then they played a game Julio made up. He called it "Bumper Bubbles." They bounced around, and when they got within an arm's distance of each other, they gently bumped off of their make-believe body-bubbles. They all ended up dropping to the ground laughing.

Laughter was extra refreshing for the Safe Peeps, especially when healing work could sometimes feel so hard. Julio acknowledged that "comedy" helped him stay in better balance! Elf could see that he was naturally playful, yet he could be so grouchy now and again.

While they rested, Elf introduced the idea of the Journal Workbook. Elf asked if anyone was interested in creating the book with her. Soon they were collaborating on which tasks each would like to take on. This delighted Elf. She was used to working hard without receiving help.

She self-consciously shared that she wanted to be the writer but would welcome help with it.

A couple of elves offered to donate their handmade paper, which they had made out of recycled paper, water, bits of leaves and flower petals. Others wanted to learn how to make paper so they'd have an ample supply to make many books. A few fairies volunteered to reprint the pages with reeds dipped into soy ink and used as pens. Nelly offered to tie the binding together with twine. Susie Q agreed to create the cover art, just as Elf had hoped.

Elf was surprised and a bit shocked that Julio said he would help Elf collect and write the content for this self-help book. His matter-of-fact statement left no one to question it. Elf didn't know if she felt more uncertainty or excitement about working with Julio on the book. Julio's input would add a whole different perspective and provide help for male survivors.

Elf mused that working with him would challenge her to speak up for herself, as he was capable and quick at speaking up. She was aware of her fear of strong-willed beings who had a habit of taking control of situations. She felt her throat tighten and had to remind her inner child that her Wise Self would navigate this relationship if inwardly she got scared. As the group chatted about how this Journal could stimulate hope and freedom through the unfolding of the reader's own creativity, Elf imagined working through some issues with Fae's help.

At their next fairy circle, Fae encouraged them to take on more individual responsibility for reclaiming their wholeness now that the group wasn't meeting as often. She provided confidence-building information for the book, and said she had co-hearts who could distribute the Workbooks to many survivors when it was finished. They all left that meeting feeling more empowered by both the inner strength they had built over time and the enthusiasm over what they aspired to create in their lives through this Journal Workbook project.

Chapter ~20~

Self-Assurance, Simplifying, and Clarity

On a warm, yet slightly breezy day, Elf and Julio met on a balcony at Fae's studio treehouse to discuss the topic for the next group session. Elf asked Julio to join her in a brief meditation to open themselves to the best direction for the book. Making this request required courage; hence, she pushed herself to risk, since she was fully committed to making this project as helpful as it could be.

Julio agreed to take time for this type of deeper consideration, though he did not really understand what difference it would make. They quieted their minds and bodies. The sound of the leaves quivering in the breeze seemed to slow down around them as well. Magical music orchestrated by the songs of the birds, the rustling of the leaves on the ground as critters scampered, and the chatter of the chipmunks elevated their hearts and minds to a space of cooperation.

When they finished meditating, Julio said he felt the presence of

TUG, an acronym for The Ultimate Guide. It surprised her when he shared that, by getting still, he had become more attuned to the project.

Hearing that made Elf smile and feel more trusting of Julio. She truly desired to collaborate well, but she was intimidated by the assertive part of Julio.

Elf shared that at times she struggled with low self-esteem. As they conversed, Julio talked a lot about himself and how his confidence was growing. Inside, Elf started feeling as if she was not important to Julio because he kept talking about himself. She decided to risk speaking directly about her need. "Julio, what I'm asking is, could you help me when my self-esteem is slipping?"

He gave her his full attention, setting his dark brown eyes on her face and asking how he could help. His response reassured her that he understood her need for affirmation, but it also made her aware of her fear—did she even deserve a male's positive attention, much less his help?

Elf asked Julio to help decide the next specific topic for the Journal Workbook. "I'd like a word or phrase that means 'confidence' or 'positive self-esteem,' to best describe what we hope the reader will gain from this topic."

"Right," said Julio, "Your attention to details, Elf, helps me focus."

They wrote out possibilities, discussed them, and decided on using the phrase "Self-Assurance." They both liked the ring to the word "assurance," because to them it provided a promise of hope. They agreed that self-assurance described a trait that survivors need in order to flourish, and wrote the following notes.

Self-Assurance

Self-assurance is the grace of feeling sure, certain, poised, and assertive—able to speak or act on what you

> want. This kind of composure serves as an invisible protection from others who might interfere or not respect boundaries. It helps you remain stable in your strong Self and not overly-sensitive to what someone else is experiencing. Self-assurance is feeling confident that it is okay to be you. It brings a balanced sense of power. When you are confident and self-assured, you respect yourself and know that you deserve respect, even if someone else is not able to honor that.

Julio shared with Elf the journaling that restored his confidence during the times he struggled most with his insecurity. A friend had recommended that, at the end of the day, he write down five things he did well or was grateful to himself for that day. "Elf, give it a try. You will probably surprise yourself with the things you take for granted about you."

Elf was touched that Julio shared his struggle and cared enough about her to suggest that she try it. Her face brightened, as if she had received a compliment. He was affirming that she could give herself permission to see the good in herself and record it as important. "Thanks for the advice Julio. I will start tonight. I think it would be helpful to include your self-gratitude practice in the Journal Workbook as well."

Elf jumped up—did a little happy dance—excited about growing her confidence and being able to experience it more often! She was elated over how free she felt when she was self-assured.

Curious, she wondered about the depression she experienced when her confidence was lacking. She asked Self what she needed to know about trusting herself or anyone else. She was eager to believe that she could take steps to assure herself when she needed it most.

Collaboratively, Elf and Julio decided to include the following notes from Fae's handouts that fit the topic of self-assurance.

ASSISTANCE TO SUPPORT YOUR INNER ELF OR FAIRY

- *Self-assurance is a belief in your own abilities that can be enhanced by invisible connections with TUG, angels, fairies, flowers, animals, or people that make you feel safe.*

- *Spend time with groups, beings, and things that help you feel secure.*

- *Build and strengthen your self-esteem by pulling your shoulders back and affirming "I am strong!"*

- *Be kind to yourself by not expecting perfection. Invite improvement from yourself and stay light about it.*

- *Gratefully acknowledge what you do well.*

- *Celebrate you and your progress in ways that build lasting fulfillment.*

- *Use your physical poise to stand and walk tall. Sense a thread at the crown of your head reaching up to connect you to your north star.*

At the next group session, once the fairy circle was formed, Julio and Elf shared their notes for the Journal Workbook project and inquired if their buddies had any examples to add.

Anika brought up something that had helped her. It bothered her when others gave her advice and seemed to impose their will on her. Their words would loop around in circles in her head. She'd get stuck in self-doubt until she focused on being in the center of the bubble that surrounded her.

Anika started doing the Bubble Play—using her hands to form

a protective bubble all around her. She envisioned others in their own bubbles. She exclaimed that when she did this, the advice and impressions of others no longer interfered the way they had, and she no longer felt intimidated. By the smile on her face, the group could see that Anika was learning self-assurance.

This led to a discussion about Simplifying and Clarity, which would be the next topics in the Journal Workbook. Julio pointed out that Simplifying and Clarity overlapped, yet others saw a need to explore each topic separately. Elf swiftly jotted down notes as the group discussed the topics. Later, Julio and Elf spent time rewriting and editing the notes and ideas.

SIMPLIFY

To simplify means approaching things in a more direct and straightforward way by creating a succinct step-by-step process. When a subject is complex, use discretion to avoid oversimplifying or eliminating important details. Make it more manageable by identifying each issue over time.

- ❖ *Deconstruct an event or a pattern into smaller pieces. This may help you decrease tension.*

- ❖ *Lower your standards. Being realistic will allow your energy to support subconscious trauma healing.*

- ❖ *Choose to relax when you feel overwhelmed. It's the kind thing to do for yourself.*

- ❖ *Find ways to create distance from an intense situation or individual.*

- ❖ *Say "No thank you" to requests or events you'd rather not be part of.*

CLARITY

Clarity allows your mind to be sharp and accurate, which brings simplicity and precision to a situation. Tell yourself the truth about what is real at this time—this could very well be the opposite of what an abuser or anyone hiding the abuse had told you.

- ❖ *Communicate details with care when helping a part of you that hurts or feels confused.*
- ❖ *Get help when you need it.*
- ❖ *Remind yourself that although it is normal to blame yourself for abuse that happened to you, abuse is never your fault.*
- ❖ *Remove guilt that was not yours. The truth is that you were an innocent child.*
- ❖ *Kindly tell the truth to your parts. You are good and your younger parts are pure and innocent. See their innocence as you would see the purity of an adorable baby.*

A fairy in the group shared that she knew a few good ways to deconstruct scenarios and realize the truth with clarity, even if others were lying. Lightheartedly, she would use art activities and body scanning to find greater truth. She explained, "You can learn to listen to your body's instinctive response in order to recognize your truth. For example, you could choose to ask, "What feels light?" to find what is true for you. This question is a secret that fairies use when we sprinkle our fairy dust. Fairy dust also helps us recognize the "light" choice. Deep breathing with curiosity brings about the same result as fairy dust!

The elves in the group were enchanted with her contribution and desired to know more. Elf, Julio, and the fairy made plans to expand on these ideas in the Journal Workbook. The whole group offered suggestions for a name for the workbook and for the time-being, chose *Magical Journal...Inspired Healing with the Fairy Realm.*

Since the group would not meet again for a month, Fae asked the group to observe how they each use Self-Assurance, Simplifying, and Clarity over the next month.

Chapter ~ 21 ~

Hands-on-Healing

At the next group meeting, Anika told the group she had a Reiki healing session with an elf who laid her hands on Anika's body to help her tune in to her emotions. She described Reiki (pronounced *Ray-key*) as a light touch where the practitioner channels positive energy to the one receiving the healing. Anika relayed, "She let me know I was in charge by giving me a choice about whether I wanted her hands on or above my body. That helped me feel safe and respected by her."

Elf disclosed that she also learned a lot from a Reiki Teacher, Mother Sage. She said Reiki helped her become aware of feelings and insights she had not been aware of. She also affirmed that the session helped her relieve a lot of stress and sadness.

Anika perked up and said, "Reiki helped me find clarity from the confused state that I had been in, aaaah....probably related to my trauma." She spoke slowly, trying to formulate words to an experience that was indescribable. "I felt like I was almost in a dream state, but I could talk and understand what the healer was saying."

Anika also shared how she promised, through Reiki, to protect her Inner Child from now on. "My Inner Child held a lot of hurt and kept the secrets locked away until it was a safe time to release them. The Reiki healer helped guide me to care for my inner parts. I used to hate my inner little girl because I blamed her—unfairly—for the terrible experiences that were imposed on her."

Pulling her shoulders back, Anika confidently looked at her friends. "Now I feel so grateful toward my little girl. She actually protected me at a very young age by locking away the suffering, so I could focus on other things. I didn't know how to deal with the abuse back then. The session helped me understand my inner young girl and cleared a lot of pain! My little girl is happy with me now and knows she can trust me; whereas, she was scared of me when I hated her."

Elf recognized the courage it took for Anika to work with the Reiki practitioner and also the courage it took to stand up for her inner child. Most of the group had never heard of Reiki before. Now they all wanted to know more about it. Fae explained that there were also other hands-on-healing practices, including *Healing Touch™*, *Access Consciousness®*, and *Somatic Movement™*.

The friends left the circle with smiles in their hearts, grateful that they had Safe Peeps and others who really understood each other, most of the time.

Fae gave Elf notes about "courage" for the next topic of *Magical Journal... Inspired Healing with the Fairy Realm.* Julio was going on a camping trip, so Elf volunteered to cover the topic and said she would ask others for help if needed. Internally, Elf sensed fear bubbling up inside of her, so she was looking forward to some alone time to contemplate courage.

The next day, Elf took her notes in hand and climbed into a hammock that was hidden underneath the umbrella-like branches of a small weeping pussy willow tree. Every spring she would admire the downy undergrowth and gently stroke its fluffed catkins. Grandma Elf had made the hammock for her, and Grandpa Elf had fastened it to a strong branch high up between the trunk and the cascading branches that appeared to float in the breeze.

Elf felt loved as the simple fabric embraced her like a loving hug. It humored her to know that her grandparents could cooperate with each other, even if it was only out of their love for her. If only— she wished— they could respect each other in that way more often.

As she lay in the woven sling, a branch swung in front of her. She carefully reached for the slender branch with her leg outstretched in the other direction as to not flip the hammock! Although she and her brother recently had a lot of fun flipping the hammock on purpose, she knew this was a time she needed to focus.

Every so often, when Elf needed to process something important, she would shift her body to get cozy-situated. Comforting herself like this was a custom that allowed her to get most connected to her Wise Self. Today, the graceful, drooping limb that held a string of catkins became a cozy-comfort item—she caressed the pussy willows in her fingers. As her skin received the tenderness from the silky buds, the sensation soothed her entire being.

Elf's hammock rocked her back and forth as she settled her head and shoulders into its comforting embrace. She allowed herself to be rocked by the swaying motion as the swinging branches danced and bounced around her. Taking a few deep breaths, she was ready to read the notes from Fae.

COURAGE

Courage is being brave even though a part of you

> *feels scared. Identify what will support you to be the best Self you can be, and risk asking others for help. Ask responsible beings who can help you. If the first ones can't help, continue reaching out to find the help that is right for you. Courage comes from an Infinite supply. Ask Source to provide all the courage you need to recover your peace of mind.*

Elf joked to herself how it seemed as a child she had more courage than commonsense. Then again, she realized that in order to survive her childhood and carry on, she didn't have any choice except to be courageous. She marveled at her courage to tell when Gerome had come to her school to teach about safe touch. She thanked her little girl part for being so amazingly brave!

Awareness arose of how other survivors deadened their pain with drugs, alcohol, or blaming and apathy. Sensitivity to her parents' dysfunction motivated her to choose courage, for the most part. She was starting to understand and own how gutsy she had been to get help. Previously, she had discounted her bravery, judging herself for feeling so fearful. Now, her body responded to the affirmations of her courage by feeling vibrantly alive, leaving her smiling. She read on about courage:

> *There are times you may want to be alone, and this can be restful and healing. There also comes a time when one is well served to courageously risk moving beyond seclusion. Playing sports, trying a new hobby, and attending classes can help develop courage and relational skills. Karate and Tae Kwon Do are martial arts that teach security and courage.*

Elf wrote in her personal journal:

> I get depressed and lonely when I spend too

much time alone. I don't have to go through this process alone. There is always hope for healing, even if I do not sense the hope. I have wise support from friends and mentors who can lead me to the glimmer of light when needed. Even fairies—as Earth Angels—come to my aid when I ask the Universe. I am ever so grateful for all of them!

A few weeks later, Julio ran up to Elf all excited about an activity he wanted to add to the topic of courage. He was still huffing and out of breath when he started explaining it to Elf. Elf didn't like it that Julio commanded so much attention. She bit her lip and decided to talk with Fae in private about how she covered up her resentment by acting polite.

Julio jabbered so quickly about the idea that it was confusing for Elf to follow. They got into a bit of a tiff because Elf thought Julio was expecting her to organize his thoughts and write about them. Elf told Julio she needed to leave and asked him if he could write his idea down for *Magical Journal*.

"Sure. I could show it to you next week. Okay?" asked Julio.

"Well, that would be great," Elf expressed with relief. She wondered if his writing would be as bewildering as his verbal description. Then, she remembered something Mother Sage had taught her about her thoughts having energy that help her attract what she expects. She decided to change her attitude so she could provide better energy support to her writing partner. She imagined they would both be pleased with Julio's undertaking.

Lo and behold, at the following meeting, Elf felt more than fortunate to have Julio as her writing partner. She discovered that he had taken the time to organize his thoughts and re-write his ideas a few times.

Julio's mom had helped him slow down to sort his thoughts and acknowledge his feelings. He quietly told Elf, with a wink and a shimmer in his eye, that his mom had taught him how to use a magic wand to clear the shame that was not his. Elf was really intrigued when he promised to fill her in at another time. For now, he was ready to share the following exercise for *Magical Journal*.

Julio's Power Animal Play

Close your eyes, sense your breathing, and ask to be shown an animal that could help you with a situation troubling you. For example, if you feel terrified, relax and allow an animal to come to you. Get curious about how this creature can show you a way to take care of your needs. It does not need to be a ferocious animal.

Animal instincts are so strong that they can assist you in connecting with your authenticity in ways you would not expect. Authenticity means being real and natural, which is very powerful. When an animal is shown to you through this activity, that animal's energy can help give you direction and keep you safe.

Julio showed her pictures of animals he had drawn in his personal journal that had helped him when he needed them. Recently, a lion had come to protect him. He even colored a picture of the lion roaring at a man who was wearing a black robe-like garment and holding his arms outstretched toward Julio's pelvis. Dark colors extended from the man's hands. These colors created an explosion-like image on Julio's body. Another picture depicted the lion coming between them, scaring the man, who then shrank to the size of an ant.

Seeing these pictures made Elf realize why Julio had seemed so jumbled when he tried to talk about his idea for an activity to add to their journal project. She had a lot of empathy for his discomfort—

acknowledging the impact of his former abuse—since he hadn't talked about it before this.

It surprised Elf to find out that Julio didn't know who the man in his picture was. She turned to look Julio in the eyes and slowly said, "Thank you for showing me the drawings. That took courage. Are you sure you want to share them in the project—*Magical Journal*—for others to see, Julio?"

Julio got choked up and needed to clear his throat as he replied, "The best way I know how to share my feelings, ahem, is in a picture. So yes, I want to share the best way I can to be of help to others."

Elf smiled, impressed with Julio and his courage to advance forward before he had all the answers. Secretly she wished to be more like that, yet she felt watchful, fearing she would be too impulsive. Then she thought to herself, "It amazes me how much I admire Julio, yet I also get so disgruntled with him!"

The two of them added more ideas with collaborative effort that flowed easily through the courage section of their project. As they wrapped up their work together, they decided that "Belonging" was the next topic for *Magical Journal.*

Elf had plans to return to the seashore the next morning, so she left to get to bed early. Tucking her notes under her pillow, she asked the fairy angel realms for guidance. She was looking forward to gathering info about belonging, because she loved the warm, fuzzy feeling that came when she was able to get close to others who cared. She grinned about having serendipitously learned from Julio. Even though it was scary at times, she wanted to learn to have wisdom about trusting herself and others.

Chapter ~ 22 ~

Water Spirits

Elf woke with the sun, excited to go to the seashore. Being at the shore brought her clarity, increasing her ability to "see" and understand greater truth. She wondered about Shelly, feeling it had been too long since she last saw her.

When she arrived, Elf was so excited about visiting Shelly at the "see-shore" that she needed to calm herself. She did that by using all of her senses. Attending to her breathing, she sensed each footstep sinking into the soft, yet gritty texture of the sand and then the cool water. Her skin tingled as the sun kissed and embraced her. These elements helped her connect with Source energy. Relaxed, she felt the presence of her Higher Self tuning in to find Shelly.

Instinctively, Elf's tiny feet took her to the shell that Shelly had made her home. The shell stayed in the general vicinity, but the waves did move it around a tad. Elf's intuition told her that something was unusual, though.

"Shell! Shelly," she called out. There was no answer. A part of Elf started to worry, especially since their last conversation was when Shelly had sounded frightened. Had Shelly disappeared? Was she all right and still alive?

Elf felt like her head was spinning, so she sat down and drank some water to gain clarity. Her Wise Self had a talk with her frantic part and asked that part to allow Self to lead this exploration. Elf felt relieved that she did not need to be in charge of figuring this out.

She chose to lie in the sand to relax. Her Self started to imagine how fulfilling it would be to find Shelly. She felt a connection to Source and absolutely knew Shelly was well and in the vicinity. Elf imagined seeing Shelly and how grateful she was for finding her. She was creating what she desired with the magic touch of advance gratitude, which was a fundamental secret of the fairy realm.

Elf was drawn to take a swim. She suspected it was her higher Self guiding her. As she walked into the ocean, she enjoyed the gentle push and pull of the waves as they danced her. Her body delighted in the ongoing rush of rhythm and movement. The exhilarating, cool temperature quickly made her feel vibrantly alive. The nourishing salt water held her and soothed her emotions until she was able to let go of all worry.

She noticed a pod of dolphins joyfully circling around water-sprites as they played in the liquid of life. The sensitive part of Elf could feel the joy rippling outward from the pod. It transmitted sensations of pleasure into her body and emotions and stirred her spirit.

Elf was curious to see if the dolphins would play with her, so she dove under to get closer. That's when she saw shimmering mermaids and mermen of all sizes, petite seahorses, and other sea creatures who were more colorful than she had ever seen. One of the water sprites spotted Elf and seemed to recognize her!

An unexpected feeling came over Elf. It was as if she knew the water sprite who approached her and gazed deep into her eyes. Elf struggled to stay under the water, but being an Elf—not a water sprite—she needed air to breathe. Just like that, a seahorse swooped to Elf's aid, lifting her above the surface, then returning her below when she was ready.

Once Elf knew she was safe, she was calm enough to get a good look at the water sprite who smiled and gazed at her. Her heart skipped...the eyes were the ones that once peered out of the shell Elf had befriended!

"Shell...Shelly, is that you?" Elf asked with her eyes, since she could not speak words that made sense underwater. Gratefully, Elf remembered how to get the impression of words when they weren't spoken, like she had with Ria, the caterpillar turned butterfly.

Feelings filled her heart that transmitted, "Yes, Elf. It is me, Shelly. I am so happy to see you." They joyously hugged as they floated to the surface.

"You arrived just in time to witness my family's Welcoming Ritual," continued Shelly. "I have been adopted by new kin-mermaids. My other parents were deemed unfit to care for me. I really belong to the kin who respect me and can best care for me. Mermaids are excellent at self-care and care of family."

Elf's salty tears of joy mingled with the surrounding salt water. Her heart gently throbbed with excitement over this miracle for Shelly as she watched the beautiful ceremony with Shelly's new parents and two brothers. They invited Elf to became part of a synchronistic water-dance that joined their hearts in the glory of sacred community. Shelly shared her gratitude for learning that true love is safe. She was starting a new life with her new supportive family.

Elf Feels Torn

Elf was eager to spend time alone with Shelly after the festivities.

Shelly had "come out of her shell" and changed in many ways. She had softened, yet she had strengthened herself, and Elf wanted to find out how she had done that.

"Shelly, I admire your courage to grow and take risks. I am simply amazed," Elf shared. Elf was genuinely sincere, but at the same time she felt envious of Shelly's family bond. Elf chose to be compassionate toward that part of her, which softened the envy.

"Thanks, Elf. I notice you seem more confident and comfortable yourself," exclaimed Shelly.

"Oh, it is really nice to hear that. I have worked so hard to heal, I didn't notice that I have improved."

Shifting her thoughts to Shelly, Elf asked, "How did you sort out your feelings about your parents? I struggle with my feelings about my parents, and my experiences were not as traumatic as yours." Yearning to learn from Shelly's healing, Elf pleaded, "Shelly, could you share how you resolved things?"

"I am happy to share with you, Elf. You helped me long ago when I had given up all hope. Let's see. Thinking back about my first foster parents seems like another lifetime. I like to think of it that way, too. Thinking of them as if that were a past life, keeps them out of my life right now.

"Sometimes I need to imagine containers like compartments to hold people and experiences at a distance. It works for me when I think of the container as an old book that holds a story from my past. I don't know whether my foster parents wanted to be part of a confusing, messy story, but they stayed in a story that felt very wrong for me. They denied their pain and chose to do things that numbed them. Material items, alcohol, and drugs were more important to them than other beings, including me."

Seeing the understanding in Elf's eyes, Shelly continued, "Elf, I can't deny the pain I felt about all the abuse. I'm grateful that social elf workers believed me and removed me from that foster family. It was the only family I knew. I'm learning to trust my new family, but I do get scared, even though they listen and care about my feelings. They tell me all my feelings are acceptable and normal, considering what I have been through. I feel like they are my real parents because they treat me with kindness and love, and they care about my safety."

Shelly asked, "Does that help you, Elf?"

"Honestly, I feel some envy. You have what I long for—a family that treats you with respect. I am glad for you but sad for me," whined Elf.

"Oh, Elf. I am sorry that you don't have a family that fully cares for you in a pure, functional way. How do you get through it?" Shelly really wanted to know.

"I look forward to being with my friends and my fairapist. They are much more like family than my family is."

"Hmmmm, Elf, could you find a way to think of your friends and supporters as your true family? Would it help if you refer to the elves in your house with words other than family?" inquired Shelly.

"Maybe," responded Elf with minor irritation and a question in her voice. "I think I need to talk this o-u-u-t and take some time to process this idea. It helped me when you said you imagine the painful story of your family as an old book. I picture that old book as one I can't discard yet, even though I don't like the entire story inside!"

Needing to talk through this with Shelly, Elf ranted, "I feel disgusted that my family could ignore my truth. Surprisingly, the disgust motivates me to move past my helplessness. I hope to use the anger constructively by commanding clarity about my association with the book—the story in it. I don't know what I want to do with the story, yet."

Talking it out cracked open her confusion. "The story shows me that my mother is stuck in drama that does not make sense to me. My father goes along with her, so he, too, is trapped there. They see no way of getting out!"

Shelly reflected back the issue by stating, "Your mom has been overly passive about the crimes that caused you immense trauma, but she over-reacts to minor details in life that don't matter. Your dad never stood up to your mother to acknowledge your truth, so he too, is over-passive about your well-being."

"Overly-passive about crimes," repeated Elf as she recognized more fully that this was their issue; not hers. "Shelly, your wording shifts this into a clearer perspective for me." Elf was wonderfully mesmerized by energy spiralling through her body relieving the angst of her overtaxed brain.

With a deep sigh, closing her eyes, and a quiver to her lips, Elf affirmed her newly discovered truth, "What if... accepting that they are stuck, frees me from hopelessly wishing they will change? Accepting they are not open to change is really a freeing choice for me. I am grateful I'm not stuck inside their story and can create a healthier life for myself, as well as be a good example for my brother." Her voice, tougher than usual, trembled as she let her body feel the grief. "What breaks my heart is that my parents can't see me for who I am and what I stand for."

"I know. Heartbreak opens the heart for something greater," said Shelly, as she reached out her arms toward Elf. "Would you like a hug?"

Elf nodded as tears welled up. Her tears streamed onto Shelly's shoulder as Elf melted into the warmth of love wrapped around her. They embraced for a long time, sealing the deep bond of friendship. Elf took in the wholehearted, nurturing energy and let it fill all of her.

Elf recognized that her heartbreak allowed her heart to open—to seek what she really needed. Her resilience turned a bitter experience to bittersweet. Elf let the bitterness fade into that old worn-out book that represented the parents she lived with and their twisted ways. Then she imagined the story in that outdated book shrinking into a teeny tiny tidbit that had little effect on her now.

In her imagination, a brand new book appeared, beaming with light. It was hers to fill with the brightest future she could imagine. She smiled contentedly and kept this new book in her heart, filling the chapters with love and kindness.

Chapter ~ 23 ~

Comfort and Belonging

Back home the next day, Elf merrily rolled and stretched her body on a carpet of fresh moss on the forest floor, reflecting on the elements of Mother Earth. She reveled in the glory of the woods, the brilliant shades of green, the soft, moss-covered ground that cradled her, and the majestic presence of the sheltering trees.

She marveled over how the ocean was a womb-like place. Its energy birthed a renewed sense of appreciation within her and all who witnessed its wonder during Shelly's Welcoming Ritual. Being underwater was like being in another world, exquisite, yet so different from where she was now.

Perhaps it was the strong bond she felt in the water kingdom that made her aware of her sense of belonging. She felt connected to the forest, the land, her brother, her friends, and the critters that scampered about.

Opening her journal, she wrote about her need to connect with others who could understand her and care about her dreams. She added gratitude for her resilient spirit. Clearly, she could see how much she had recovered from the trauma in her life when she was able to share—even her turmoil—with Shelly.

Later that day, a few of the Safe Peeps got together to design more of *Magical Journal*. This is a smidgen of what they came up with after an interesting conversation.

BELONGING

Belonging is a sense of fitting together or joining, as in feeling accepted by others or welcome in a certain place. Ideally, it is an advantageous relationship for all involved. Overall, if it is not mutually satisfying and does not feel emotionally safe, it is best to step back to give room for potential trust to grow. A healthy sense of belonging allows you to be yourself, and you feel stronger for it. Groups create a sense of community in the form of a support group, club, clan, or tribe.

It is helpful to allow this sense of joining with others to change and fluctuate. The winds of change have a purposeful role in nature. Dance with the winds and care for yourself as your needs require, recognizing that you, too, are an important part of nature.

Imagine playing "connect the dots", connecting to the people, places and things that help you feel safe. Connection can deepen the warm feeling of belonging. Imagine energetically getting in-sync, somewhat like puzzle pieces come together.

Can you connect to your Creator/your inner TUG/ the Source that gives life energy? Your Creator can help your Self feel strong to connect with your parts. Pause now and breathe in that expansion of Self. Close your eyes and let your Wise Self soak in comforting light. It may just be a spark at first.

Allow that light to expand with each inhale. Feel how beautiful it is to connect with your Source. Know that Source is always here for you. People have different names for their Source. Some refer to the all-knowing energy as God, Goddess, the Force, the Universe, TUG— The Ultimate Guide, or White Light. Use the name that has meaning for you. Honor what you believe or what feels light to you.

Source, Radiating to Self and Elf

After leaving the Safe Peeps, Elf colored a picture that supported her young part. It was a symbol of her whole Self and the Divine energy that is always there providing for her. A ball of light glowed from Source, radiating to Self and Elf, filling the whole page. She sensed the gifts of Self coming through Elf—herself.

Source

Self

Elf

Elf picked up a leaflet Fae had given her and read:

> *Sometimes terrifying, confusing experiences have scared a part away from our whole Self. It is an illusion that our parts are separate from our TUG. We can 're-member' them by re-uniting Self with the wholeness—the positive intent—hidden inside each part. Update your part with the information that it is not alone. Inner re-connection restores your wholeness.*

Elf marveled that this is what she had learned in fairapy with Fae. She made notes to offer exercises like this in the project, *Magical Journal*.

COMFORT

Elf decided that the topic 'comfort' fit well with belonging. She wrote: **"It is a gift and a comfort to have outside resources—as a group to belong to—when it strengthens our own inner connection."** She reflected on her desire to comfort her feelings when they needed it most, creating an inner sense of attachment to her Wise Self.

There were times when Elf's parts demanded attention all at once, and it overwhelmed her. When she reflected quietly, she realized that she could not help all of her parts all of the time. Wanting them to know that she would get to each of them when she could, first she gave them gratitude for the important information they could provide. She then asked her dear parts to please be patient with her and, subsequently, felt calmness grow inside. They curled up with her and asked her to call them "elfie". With a tear in her eye, she was moved to enter this important letter in her own journal:

Letter to My Younger Elfie

My Dear, Dear Parts, My desire is to remember you and truly see the pure goodness inside of you. I am sorry that you experienced so much turmoil, shame, and pain in the past. I want you to know the abuse is over and not happening any more. My wish is to acknowledge your suffering, tenderly comfort your tension, and free you to enjoy a life of awareness and pleasure. I respect all of your feelings and invite you to release emotions when you and I are ready.

I love you. I trust you. I forgive you. I care deeply about you. Please let me know how I can nourish you and assist your Self growth. Between us there is nothing but love. I accept and approve of you. I imagine you coming back into wholeness.

I can now choose beings to support and help me, when I need it. Grace fills my life and creates a life I enjoy more and more. I take time to care for you—my parts, by connecting to my Wise Self. I choose to learn what is best for me and nurture our growth.

Love Always,

Elf

Chapter ~ 24 ~

Lighten Up

Another Self-quality that Julio came up with and introduced in the fairy circle was Comedy. The Safe Peeps talked about choosing comedy at the right time to bring in a lightness that rejuvenates the soul. They recognized that humor often shifted the group's energy when they got too serious. In fact, the entire fairy realm found great delight in clowning and amusement. Some of them are known for being tricksters just for the sake of fun.

Loving Laughter

Elf attended a Laughter Yoga Class with her brother, Bevin, and a few of her woodland friends. They became friends with others in the class as they did many simple exercises together that made them giggle and sometimes had them bursting into full-out laughter.

When the class had started, Elf had been feeling troubled about life. When it was over, she not only felt lighter, but she also felt self-assured and hopeful. "HA, HA, HO, HO. HO," vibrantly rang through her head!

She learned that she could laugh for no reason and remembered a time long ago when she often did just that. Now, she knew she could initiate a sense of joy to spark laughter and laugh just for the fun of it. She discovered that laughter is contagious, and especially enjoyed how the lark of laughter from others made her laugh harder.

Elf and Bevin decided to make laughter a regular practice. Their laughter brought an enchanting spirit of delight into their everyday family life. The joyful sounds made their parents curious, smile more, and even chuckle.

Unbeknownst to humans, the fairy realm is drawn to people's laughter and often adds to the energy of laughter. You can be certain that fairies are present when a person cannot control their laughing.

Appropriate Time for Laughter

Elf reflected on times when she felt too disturbed to laugh. She'd learned to be discerning and know when it was not the right timing for her to focus on laughing. This had been a discussion with Fae and the Safe Peeps when they realized that many of them used laughter to cover up pain—which was not helpful for healing.

The group had also acknowledged that using anything to cover pain did not make it go away. In fact, when they buried their pain inside, it seemed to grow. Fae taught them that pain needs the right time and place to be released, so that all emotions can be heard and tended to constructively. Elf mentioned that as she releases her pain, it makes room for her desired feelings.

The group conversed about difficult times in which they had been laughed at because they made a mistake, and times when their feelings were hurt because someone had made fun of some part of their body. The group was applying what they'd learned about discernment—

being careful to choose appropriate times to laugh. Fae mentioned that pleasure is a fulfilling sensation only if it does not harm anyone.

Elf made a new friend in class whose name was Bailey. He was a tall, blonde-haired fairy who laughed often. Elf hung out with him a lot because she found herself laughing more when she was around Bailey. They would read jokes, or make up their own, and giggle until they were giddy. Bailey even introduced laughter exercises to Elf's parents. Their willing participation surprised Elf, and helped her view them in a new way.

Sharing happiness brought Elf balance to counter the pain she had processed, leaving her feeling very content and centered. Just knowing she could return to sheer pleasure helped her accept and move through sorrow more quickly when it did come up.

After that, Elf asked her friends to do a "laughter exercise" when things felt too serious or she was bored. Her favorite was one she made up, called The Funny Bone Dance. They would all start by moving a bone in their body and acting as if it made them chuckle. Moving more bones would increase their laughter until their bodies were bouncing and dancing while making hilarious sounds. The more folks who joined, the longer the merriment lasted.

The laughter game was one way in which Elf was able to connect with her relatives. It drew Elf closer to Bevin, even though they irritated one another now and again. The laughter seemed to erase their need to revert to some of the annoying habits they used to avoid being honest about their feelings.

Elf's Laughter Yoga practice taught Elf she could bring this lighter energy into any situation she desired. The younger elf part that once carried so many burdens wished to play the part of Elf's muse. A muse is one who whimsically inspires another for fun and joy. Elf noticed more grace, joy, and ease because of her muse. She called on her Inner

Muse when lightening up was beneficial. Elf and Julio also called on their muses to help construct pages for *Magical Journal*, making it a fun book.

Elf made time to honor other feelings, too. Acknowledging the truth and moving through her feelings allowed more freedom for Self to make choices. Lightening up helped her accept her feelings, which changed how she related with others. Her most important relationships gradually improved when she experienced more joy. Elf knew she could choose humor and still have other feelings—there was now space for both.

Best of all, Elf continued to learn how to love and respect her life more! Her "Self" taught all her child parts that her body and mind are intended to be treated as sacred. Touch of her body needed to feel right to her—if it didn't, she had the right to refuse touch from another. She had authority to make the decision about how she would be touched and treated and by whom. Her body, emotions, thoughts, and spirit were meant to enjoy pleasure.

Delightfully, Elf cultivated that pleasure with safe touch, movement, and dance. She also generated pleasure by journaling her feelings, writing positive ideas about herself, and choosing to do what she loved, especially playing in nature. She noticed hummingbirds—representing the sweetness and joy of life—hovering around her more often. When it was not possible for her to seek pleasure, she would do what she could to relieve pain and move toward increasing her joy.

Elf used her sensitivity and awareness to uplift others in the fairy realm and beyond. She hoped her example of integrity and positive energy would help to change the world. She longed for it to become a safe place some day for everyone.

Elf knew that Her Wise Self had unlimited resources, both in the world and within her heart and mind. She had learned from Mother

Sage that each generation would now bring in new awareness, better boundaries, and healing possibilities for those who had been abused and also for those who violated others. Putting a voice to the right for every child to be safe brought attention to the need for communities to develop plans to protect the children of the future. A great change had begun, and support was growing to assist in ending childhood abuse.

Chapter ~ 25 ~

The Welcomed End

Fae invited her group to gather for an important meeting. During this meeting she wanted to acknowledge the Safe Peeps for the array of contributions they were adding to beings in the world. She also invited me, Badger, to the meeting to give an update of some hopeful news.

The group created a fairy ring amidst a circle of mushrooms, and Fae encouraged all to share what they were creating or adding to life. She fully acknowledged everyone's participation, and affirmed them for their growing ability to "be their true self" and to live in as much peace and joy as one is able.

Elf and Julio each shared their current aspirations for their project of *Magical Journal*. Elf was very clear about her desire to share with other survivors what she was learning about herself. She shined in her role as a co-creator. Julio spoke proudly, holding his chin high, knowing he was part of something so meaningful. He accentuated his observation of the lack of support for males and the lack of conversation between males about such topics.

I saw that Julio indeed was an activist wanting to provide what males needed to create support amongst each other. At that moment, his hutzpah sparked an interest in me to inquire if he would share his story and challenges in another book to follow this one.

"If you would narrate the story, Badge"—he nicknamed me as if we were suddenly best buds—"I reckon I would," Julio fired back.

"This is gonna be fun!" I responded, recognizing I may have met my match with a bit of a wild side.

Elf enthusiastically added gratitude for Julio's perspective on their shared project and for the help provided by the rest of the group. She exclaimed, "This book project is so fulfilling. I hope you, too, will follow what brings your heart deep gratification."

One by one, each elf and fairy shared what feeling and state of being enlivened their spirit. They discussed how being their true selves impacted the earth. Gratitude flowed as the thriving souls expressed their wonderment to have been a part of such an inspiring journey with each another. One fairy exclaimed that she had learned so much it was hard to even remember the place where they started. Everyone agreed that it was a memorable journey to be grateful for!

When they were finished sharing, I, Badger, gave them exciting news. I told them, "Because so many fairy folk who were abuse survivors have reclaimed their self-love and personal power—over half of the survivors—it has created a tremendous energy shift in this world. This change influenced the justice system in the fairy realms, and led them to remedy the wrong behavior of the sex offenders.

"It started in this way: I, along with others, reported the facts about the crimes of the offenders. Other animal friends were given the authority to chase the criminals off our land and onto an island that houses a prison for the offenders. The law took over and regulated an appropriate length of confinement for the offenders and mandated that they attend sex offender treatment and education classes.

"These actions led to a Restorative Justice Program that understood how the long-term effects of sexual abuse impact not only the victim, but also those who are in relationship with the victim. It recognized the need to offer a safe place for victims and the victim's family and friends to express the pain they suffered. Offenders were required to witness their victim's accounts of the tormented feelings and confusion caused by the sexual abuse.

"Through this recovery program, offenders were set on a path of atoning for their wrongdoing. Most became accountable and remorseful. Many developed empathy and wanted to set things right for the betterment of the community. They admitted their abusive behavior. They acknowledged understanding how they had harmed their victims. They grieved how their wrongdoing had caused such long-lasting trauma for their victims and their families.

"The remorseful offenders committed to taking every step necessary to prevent themselves and others from ever violating any other being. One of the steps involved converting their negative, dark impulses into positive, wise choices to live with integrity and self-control. Some characters stubbornly remained in denial of having violated anyone, felt no empathy toward their victims, and gained few privileges in jail.

"Most of the pedophiles (sex offenders of children) connected with the Nature Spirits to identify their own childhood wounding and how they used abusive behaviors to avoid feeling their own hurt and fear. It is a long process for them to stop reverting to power and control behaviors when they become aware of their feelings, especially guilt and shame.

Through the Restorative Justice Program, communities hope to be successful at preventing sexual abuse from ever occurring among the fairy realm again. They mandated that, even though pedophiles learn appropriate boundaries, they are not allowed to be alone around children, ever. The remorseful pedophiles were able to recognize abusive character traits in others and confronted them before they acted out."

After I, Badger, finished reporting the important news, the group acknowledged that many fairies are dedicated to guiding humans to end the cycle of sexual abuse. They know it can be done, and they offer assistance to souls who are open to ask the Universe for help. It is one way the Universe assists creatures as they progress toward a better way of life for all. It is usually the survivor's yearning for restoration that calls on the Earth Angels—including the fairies—for help in more ways than they imagine. As the victim-survivor heals, the energy directed toward justice builds, opening the way for a safer future.

The work that all of you have done to share your growth in healing is a great way for this energy to build, too! Awareness and fairness is increasing every year, month, and day, even though it may not seem apparent yet. Can you imagine…a world where children's bodies and rights are respected? The fairy folk are prompting all kinds of messages for healing, self-love, and empowerment. The fairies often sing a song they once whispered to John Lennon: "Imagine…all the people…living life in peace."

Ria floated in on a breeze and asked us to imagine what could be possible if enough dreamers and advocates envision what is needed and take action to end childhood sexual abuse. As her wings gracefully lowered and rose, she reminded us in her silent song that love responds to needs.

About Empowerment

I also shared with the group that long, long ago females and sex were regarded as especially sacred. After some group conversation, I continued the story, "Males and females were respectful and respected. Picture a time—free of abuse—when everyone is able to stay connected to their TUG and be considerate of all others."

A multitude of Nature Spirits have imagined a safe planet and taken action to create a new reality. Imagination is powerful. The more healing that takes place for each being, the more potential there is for others to recover. Being true to one's Self is also powerful! I give infinite credit and praise for survivors who have started to clear a path in the jungle of healing from sexual abuse. That start makes it easier for other survivors to venture further through recovery.

Together, the clearing and sharing inspires beings to anticipate living free from the burdens. Yet, this happens one breath at a time and one process at a time, as each chooses. Pleasure and delight are increased in the same way, which elevates survivors to become thrivers. You, as thrivers, have learned that life, for the most part, is meant to be a truly delightful experience, and you are learning to live that way.

Fae chimed in to add, "All of you—the Angelic Fairy Realm, along with Mother Sage and Badger—have infused restorative energies into this story, so that all who read or listen to these words will be immersed in nature's resources, which will continue to rebuild their spirit, emotions, mind, and body."

And so it is.

References

Levine, Peter A., PhD (2003) Sexual Healing -Calm the Panic- session two, exercise 5: Finding Safety in the Body, with permission from Sounds True, Inc. Boulder, CO: Sounds True.

Schwartz, Richard C., PhD (2001) Introduction to the Internal Family Systems Model, with permission- Oak Park, IL: Trailheads Publications.

Resources

Visit Katiacooper.com for links to more resources.

About the Cover Artist

Bettina Madini is an artist, singer, bestselling author, coach and inspiring speaker.

With a career in both the corporate and the art world Bettina invites the world to discover what true living might be. She uses her creativity to demonstrate that we can create the life we truly desire. To find more about her painting and creativity retreats, online programs, coaching sessions, silk paintings and designer garments, please visit www.BettinaMadini.com.

Acknowledgements

I whole-heartedly shower gratitude on everyone who has contributed to the emergence of this book! Thank you for your shared desire that others flourish with this project.

I am forever grateful to my husband, Don, for your long-term love, support and honoring of my time on this project. Life with you is an exciting adventure!

For my courageous clients and students who have shared from the depths of your souls, thank you for trusting me. You inspire me to keep growing and to continue creating inspiration.

Dear Sara Daleiden, I feel deeply gifted by your insights, your authenticity, and your support. I so admire your devotion to your self-discipline to creating a better world!

Tremendous gratitude to you, Jodie Ellis-Hart, for your enthusiasm and encouragement that helped move me forward when it was most challenging.

Marilyn Hein, I can't imagine an Earth Angel more dedicated to the editing process than you provided! You helped this story flow like a comforting, bubbling brook. Your ability to listen deeply to undercurrents has been a generous gift.

Anna Casper, thank you for being the reliable, sincere friend who shows up when I need yet another miracle talent that I didn't know you had. Your input and touch to this project brought a completeness.

Sweet Maria Weeks! The editing magic you have with ideas helped this story blossom. Your curiosity stretched my communication to authentically touch more readers. I am grateful for you.

Cindy Smith, it all started with you, when I shared my dream for this book and more. Thank you for believing in me and offering your caring guidance when my writing started in a raw, chaotic state.

Kira Henschel with Henschel Haus Publishing, Inc., you were the first editor to pull a lot of weeds and lay more of the groundwork for this garden. I so admire your gifts and generous heart!

For the joy of Winalee Zeeb. Your regenerating brave, open heart that dances so fully in life continues to inspire me in countless ways! You not only taught me how to teach and live Nia (the joy of movement), your acceptance and deep caring taught me how to allow that for myself and others.

To the beloved Nancy Retzlaff, my dear friend and spiritual teacher. I have been transformed by your love for life and for others. Most gratefully, I still receive your guidance and love from the other side.

A shout-out for the Book Mama and the Beautiful Writers Group. Genius Mama! Gratitude for bringing our tribe together. Generous. Inspiration. Connection!

To the wizard of Happy Publishing, Erica Glessing. Your light and laughter is the butterfly that floats worry away. Thank you for your patience and your ability to elevate the process allowing this book to fly.

For Bettina Madini, the fairy artist, extraordinaire! I appreciate your magic mentoring and your creative touch to this book cover.

Special thanks to Donna *Faye* Roidt, my fairy-elf helper for allowing me more time to devote to this book.

My dearest friends, healing practitioners and therapists, you know who you are. I am infinitely blessed by all you have shared. I am very grateful. Anne Smith, your healing intentions and book guidance have been an extra bonus.

Our grown children, Charles and Kristen, and your families... you are all tremendous gifts and you make my life sparkle! I cherish your love, humor, and patience with me. Lindsey, I continue to learn about ease from you. Matt, thank you for your assistance with this project.

To my Inner Child, for your connection to the nature spirits, your bravery and wildly-creative spirit. I am infinitely blessed with you.